THOUGHTS

&

Notions

High Beginning Reading Practice

Linda Lee
Barbara Bushby

HH **Heinle & Heinle**
Thomson Learning™

Australia • Canada • Denmark • Japan • Mexico • New Zealand • Philippines
Puerto Rico • Singapore • South Africa • Spain • United Kingdom • United States

The publication of *Thoughts & Notions* was directed by the members of the ESL/EFL team at Heinle & Heinle:

Editorial Director: Erik Gundersen
Marketing Development Director: Charlotte Sturdy
Assistant Editor: Jill Kinkade
Sr. Manufacturing Coordinator:
  Marybeth Hennebury
Production Services Coordinator:
  Maryellen Killeen

Director of Global ESL Trng. & Development:
  Evelyn Nelson
Associate Marketing Development Director:
  Marianne Bartow
Compositor: PC&F, Inc.
Vice President and Publisher: Nancy Leonhardt
Photoresearcher: Jeffery M. Freeland

Photograph Credits: Jonathan Stark, Image Resource Director, Heinle & Heinle Publishers

For permission to use material from this text, contact us:

web   www.thomsonrights.com
fax   1-800-730-2215
phone   1-800-730-2214

Library of Congress Cataloging-in-Publication Data
Lee, Linda
        Thoughts & Notions : high beginning reading practice / Linda Lee,
Barbara Bushby.
        p.   cm.
    Includes indexes.
    ISBN 0-8384-8222-8
    1. English language Textbooks for foreign speakers.   2. Reading
comprehension--Problems, exercises, etc.   3. Readers.   I. Bushby,
Barbara.   II. Title.   III. Title: Thoughts and notions.
PE1128.L427 1999
428.6'4--dc21   99-34946
                                                              CIP

Manufactured in the United States of America
10 9 8 7 6 5 4 3 2 1
Heinle & Heinle Publishers
20 Park Plaza
Boston, MA 02116

Contents

Thoughts & Notions is a high-beginning reading skills text designed for students of English as a second or foreign language who know the basic structures of English and who have a vocabulary of roughly 800 English words. This text teaches about 1200 more words. The text groups twenty-five highly engaging reading selections into five themes of universal interest.

Thoughts & Notions is one in a series of three reading skills texts. The complete series has been designed to meet the needs of students from the beginning to the intermediate level and includes the following:

- *Facts & Figures, Third Edition* . . . . beginning

- *Thoughts & Notions* . . . . high beginning

- *Cause & Effect, Third Edition* . . . . intermediate

In addition to the student text, there is also an instructor's manual, video cassette and audio cassette available for *Thoughts & Notions*. The instructor's manual contains answers to all the exercises, a test for each unit, strategies for using news video in the classroom and transcriptions of each video clip. The audio cassette contains recordings of each of the twenty five readings in the text.

• **Theme-based approach to reading.** Each of the five units has a theme, such as sports, food, or business. The beginning lessons have a text that is about one page long. The length gradually increases to a little more than one page. The texts in the first unit are purposely easy and cover information the students already know, so that with this comparatively easy material, they can get used to the book, the class, and the instructor.

• **Systematic presentation and recycling of vocabulary.** One of the primary tasks of beginning students is developing a useful and personally relevant vocabulary base. In *Thoughts & Notions*, about twelve words are introduced in each lesson. These words appear in boldface type. Underlined words are illustrated or glossed in the margin. All of the new vocabulary items are used several times in the lesson and then are systematically recycled throughout the text. All the words introduced in the text are listed in the Vocabulary Index located in the back of the book.

● **Pedagogical Design.** The central goal of *Thoughts & Notions* is to help students develop the critical reading skills they will need for academic, personal, and/or career purposes. Toward this end, each unit offers a comprehensive program that begins with pre-reading questions, continues with reading and discussion, and proceeds through a set of carefully sequenced post-reading exercises.

Rationale for Various Exercise Types

● **Context Clues.** A context clue exercise at the beginning of each unit introduces some of the vocabulary for that unit. This section is designed to pre-teach particularly important vocabulary items.

● **Pre-reading Questions.** These questions provide a motivation for reading the text. Some are yes/no questions that can be answered by looking carefully at the visual. They are designed simply to call to mind whatever knowledge of the subject the student may already have. Through close scrutiny of the visual, the student begins to draw conclusions, putting logical reasoning into play. Some of the questions cannot be answered before the text is read. Students can look for the answers to these questions while reading the text. Some questions require student input and opinions.

● **Vocabulary.** The first exercise has sentences taken directly from the text. All new words are included. This is for practice in reading the sentences again and writing the new words.

● **Vocabulary (new context).** This exercise gives further practice with the new words in a different context but with the same meaning.

● **Vocabulary Review.** Vocabulary items are used in subsequent texts and exercises to give additional review. They are fill-ins or matching synonyms and antonyms.

● **Comprehension.** These are either true/false, true/false/no information, or multiple choice. There are also inference and discussion questions marked with an asterisk.

- **Questions.** These comprehension questions are taken directly from the text. They can be done orally in class, and/or the students can write the answers as homework. Those marked with an asterisk are either inference or discussion questions.

- **Main Idea.** Students must choose the main idea of the text from three possibilities.

- **Word Study.** A word study section is provided at the end of each unit. It reinforces structural points, such as verb forms, pronouns, and comparison of adjectives, that the students are learning in other classes. It also gives spelling rules for noun plurals and verb endings. Later units have charts of word forms. The exercises are not intended to be complete explanations and practice of the grammar points. The material in this section is included in the tests in the instructor's manual.

- **Writing.** Each unit closes with an optional writing exercise that the instructor may assign. The students may be asked to write answers to one, two, or all three of these questions.

- **Extension Activities.** Each unit ends with a four-page collection of high-interest, interactive tasks to help students practice the new vocabulary and the skills they have learned in more open-ended contexts.

New Features in the Third Edition

- **Audio Cassette.** Recordings of all the readings are provided on tape. This allows students who have not yet mastered sound/letter correspondence the opportunity to listen to the readings. In general, students will be able to better understand the pronunciation of new vocabulary.

- **Extension Activities.**
  - **CNN** Video Activity—The highlight of each set of Extension Activities is a short video-based lesson centered on a stimulating, authentic clip from the CNN video archives. Each video lesson follows the same sequence of activities:

- *Before You Watch* encourages students to recall background knowledge based on their own experiences or from information presented in the readings.
- *As You Watch* asks for students to watch for general information such as the topic of the clip.
- *After You Watch* gets students to expand on the main points of the video clip by establishing further connections to the reading passages, their own experiences and their ideas and opinions.

- **Activity Page**—Games found on this page encourage students to practice the vocabulary and structures found in that unit's lessons in a relaxed, open-ended way.
- **Dictionary Page**—Exercises on this page offer students practice with dictionary skills based on entries from *The Basic Newbury House Dictionary.*

- **Skills Index.** This index provides teachers and students with a handy reference for reading and writing skills as well as grammatical structures found in the text.

Teaching Methods

After the class studies the introductory illustration and accompanying pre-reading questions, the teacher may choose to either read the text aloud or ask students to read it silently. Then the class can do the exercises, with the instructor or students writing the answers on the board. For variety, the students might do the exercises together in small groups. Then the class as a whole can go over the exercises quickly.

Students need to understand the subject matter so they can answer the comprehension and main idea questions, but they should not be required to learn the information. It should be stressed to the students that the purpose of *Thoughts & Notions* is to teach reading skills and vocabulary, not information. Otherwise, they will be spending hours memorizing facts that they do not need to know.

Since students are not required to learn the information presented in the readings, they can go through the book fairly quickly. It is probably necessary to go through the first unit slowly, but after that, we suggest that the students do about one lesson together in class and one as homework each day. The students can do a lesson together in class. The instructor can then introduce the pre-reading questions and read the next text, assigning that lesson for homework. The next day, he or she can go over the assignment in class and introduce, read, and assign another. Students should read each text two or three times as homework. At the end of each lesson, they should test themselves on the boldface vocabulary items and memorize any words that they have not learned through use.

Students should learn all of the material in the word study sections. It is all basic material that they need to know. The explanations are purposely very simple so that students can easily understand them. Most instructors will want to give further explanations as they present each part.

There is ample material for class discussions if the text is used in conjunction with a spoken English class. Alternatively, if students are enrolled in an intensive reading skills course, there is no need to discuss the content of the lessons, except to verify comprehension.

There are no timed readings. Students should be allowed to read at their own speed so that they have time to notice everything they possibly can about the English language.

Instructor's Manual

The student text for *Thoughts & Notions* is accompanied by a comprehensive instructor's manual. This teacher's component includes pedagogical notes, a section titled "Using Authentic News Video in the ESL/EFL Classroom," transcriptions of the CNN video clips, an answer key for the student text, and tests for each of the five units presented in *Thoughts & Notions*.

The unit tests include a new reading selection with comprehension and main idea questions, general questions on the reading selections in the unit, and questions on the exercise material in the book. Each test has twenty to thirty questions. The students should be able to do the tests in about ten to fifteen minutes, allowing a half minute for each item. There is also a short quiz on the first two lessons for instructors who want to test their students during the first week or two of classes.

Acknowledgements

The authors and publisher would like to thank the following individuals who offered helpful feedback and suggestions for the development of this text:

- Virginia Heringer – Pasadena City College (CA)
- Greg Keech – City College of San Francisco (CA)
- Yvonne Sullivan – Cañada College (CA)
- Caro Leather – Miami-Dade Community College (FL)
- Diane Ruggiero – Broward Community College – Central Campus (FL)
- Kent Sutherland – Cañada College (CA)
- Ann-Marie Hadzima – National Taiwan University (Taiwan)
- Lida Baker – University of California, Los Angeles – Extension (CA)
- Mark Rossiter – ILC Pacific (Japan)
- Artela Hughes – Oak Grove High School (CA)
- Sara Storm – Orange Coast College (CA)
- Annette Fruehan – Orange Coast College (CA)

To the Student

There are many advantages of learning English. One is that you can read information about thousands of subjects. There is more information printed in English than in any other language. In this book, you will read about some of the topics that are found in English language magazines, newspapers, and books. You can also learn a lot about the world. At the same time, you will increase your knowledge of English.

Inventions and Inventors

Context Clues

Put a circle around the letter of the best answer.

1. Tony and Ann got married three years ago. Then they started fighting a lot. Now the couple are living **apart.** They live in different apartments.
   a. above
   b. among
   c. not together
   d. agree

2. Ali put a **strip** of paper in his book so he could remember what page he was on.
   a. heavy piece
   b. dark piece
   c. long thin piece
   d. dirty piece

3. There is a **row** of trees along each side of our street.
   a. line
   b. forest
   c. jungle
   d. beard

4. Half a **dozen** eggs is six eggs.
   a. fourteen
   b. twelve
   c. eight
   d. sixteen

5. Paper is **flexible.** Wood and stone are not **flexible.**
   a. You can pick it up.
   b. You can carry it.
   c. You can move it back and forth.
   d. You can hit it.

6. The paper carrier **delivers** a newspaper to my apartment every morning. I don't have to go out and buy one.
   a. hurries
   b. brings
   c. defeats
   d. buys

7. I tried to pay the government worker for helping me. She didn't **accept** the money. The government pays her and she didn't want my money.
   a. bring
   b. shoot
   c. take
   d. suppose

8. Sam **received** a package from his parents yesterday. It was a birthday present.
   a. brought
   b. got
   c. spent
   d. told

9. Stop talking **immediately!** The test started five minutes ago.
    a. soon
    b. possibly
    c. daily
    d. right now

10. Mr. Brown is a **pilot** for British Airways. He flies airplanes all over the world.
    a. businessman
    b. carpenter
    c. driver of an airplane
    d. writer for a newspaper

11. There are no classes this afternoon. You have no homework. You can do **whatever** you like.
    a. anything
    b. anywhere
    c. anytime
    d. anyone

12. Saudi Arabia has a desert **climate.** Canada has a cold **climate** in winter. The **climate** in Indonesia is tropical.
    a. the way the weather is all the time
    b. the changes in the weather every day
    c. hot and dry
    d. snow and ice

The Zipper

LESSON

1

Pre-reading Questions

1. Are you wearing a zipper?

2. What do you do when you break your zipper?

3. Do you have clothing without zippers? How does it close?

The Zipper

The **zipper** is a wonderful invention. How did people ever live without zippers? They are very common, so we forget that they are wonderful. They are very strong, but they open and close very easily. They come in many colors and sizes.

In the 1890s, people in the United States wore high shoes with a long **row** of buttons. Women's clothes often had rows of buttons too. People wanted an easier way to put on and take off clothes.

line

Whitcomb L. Judson invented the zipper in 1893. He was an engineer in Chicago. He called the zipper a **slide fastener.** However, it didn't stay closed very well. This was **embarrassing**, and people didn't buy many of them. Then Dr. Gideon Sundback from Sweden solved this problem.

A zipper has three parts: 1. There are **dozens** of metal or plastic **hooks** (called *teeth*) in two rows. 2. These are fastened to two **strips** of cloth. The cloth strips are **flexible.** They **bend** easily. 3. A fastener slides along and fastens the hooks together. When it slides the other way, it takes the hooks **apart.**

a dozen = 12

Dr. Sundback put the hooks on the strips of cloth. The cloth holds all the hooks in place. They don't come apart very easily. This solved the problem of the first zippers.

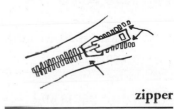

zipper

A Vocabulary

Put the right word in the blanks. The sentences are from the text.

zipper	embarrassing	hooks	dozens
sizes	fastener	flexible	slide
bend	apart	strips	row

1. In the 1890s, people in the United States wore high shoes with a long _____ of buttons.
2. There are _____ of metal or plastic _____ (called *teeth*) in two rows.
3. The _____ is a wonderful invention.
4. The cloth strips are _____.
5. He called the zipper a _____ _____.
6. When it slides the other way, it takes the hooks _____.
7. This was _____ and people didn't buy many of them.
8. They _____ easily.
9. These are fastened to two _____ of cloth.

B Vocabulary (new context)

Put the right word in the blanks.

embarrassed	strips	flexible	zippers
hooks	rows	fasteners	bend
apart	dozen	slide	size

1. Icy roads are dangerous because cars _____ on them.
2. Pam cut a piece of paper into _____.
3. Sometimes your face gets red when you feel _____.
4. A pencil is not _____. Paper is.
5. People catch fish with _____.
6. Hooks, buttons, and zippers are all _____.
7. American supermarkets sell eggs by the _____.
8. Tony and George had an apartment together, but now they live _____.
9. Students sit in a circle in some classes. They sit in _____ in others.
10. You _____ your knees when you sit down.
11. Most pants and jackets have _____.

C Vocabulary Review

Put the right word in the blanks.

leaves	axe	froze	spirits
map	shells	might	history
canoe	Current	over	death
navy	jungle	independent	shoot

1. Mary's father was in the ___ ___ ___ for twenty years.
2. Did you ever cut wood with an ___ ?
3. What time does the meeting begin, and when will it be ___ ?
4. Carl put water in the freezer part of the refrigerator. It ___ .
5. Giraffes live in grasslands. Some tigers live in the ___ .
6. Carlos had to go back to his country because of a ___ in his family.
7. Most trees have hundreds of ___ .
8. The Labrador ___ brings cold water from eastern Canada to the east coast of the United States.
9. Students usually have to memorize dates when they study ___ .
10. Ann and Paula took a long ___ trip on a quiet river during their vacation.
11. Tom is very ___ . He likes to think and do things for himself.
12. Soldiers have to learn to ___ guns.

D Comprehension

Put a circle around the letter of the best answer.

1. Zippers open and close by ___ .
   a. shooting   b. sliding   c. bending   d. choosing

2. The hooks are ___ .
   a. plastic   b. metal   c. cloth   d. a and b

3. Mr. Judson was an ___ .
   a. engineer   b. inventor   c. American   d. a, b, and c

4. Mr. Judson didn't sell many zippers because ___ .
   a. it was hard to open and close them
   b. people liked rows of buttons
   c. they came open very easily
   d. they had cloth strips

5. Dr. Sundback was _____.
   a. a Swede   b. from Chicago   c. an American   d. b and c

6. A zipper has two _____ of cloth.
   a. rows   b. fasteners   c. strips   d. buttons

7. _____ are flexible.
   a. The hooks   c. The fasteners
   b. The rows of buttons   b. The strips of cloth

8. Dr. Sundback _____.
   a. invented the zipper   c. invented the button hook
   b. made the zipper better   b. invented the slide fastener

E   Questions

The asterisk (*) means you have to think of the answer. You cannot find it in the text.

1. Why do we forget that zippers are wonderful?
2. Are zippers strong?
3. What kind of shoes did Americans wear in the 1890s?
4. Who invented the zipper? When did he invent it?
*5. Why is *slide fastener* a good name for a zipper?
6. Why were the first zippers embarrassing?
7. What country was Dr. Sundback from?
8. Describe a zipper. How does it work?
9. What part of the zipper is flexible?
10. What did Dr. Sundback do to make zippers better?
*11. What is a newer kind of fastener than the zipper?

F   Main Idea

Which is the main idea of this chapter? Choose one.

1. A zipper has hooks, cloth strips, and a slide fastener.
2. People didn't like the first zippers.
3. Mr. Judson and Dr. Sundback gave us a wonderful invention, the zipper.

The Postage Stamp

Pre-reading Questions

LESSON

2

1. Does someone in the class have a postage stamp? What does it look like?

2. Do you write letters to your relatives? Do you call them on the telephone? Which is more expensive?

3. Name a famous person on a postage stamp.

2

The Postage Stamp

Before the invention of the **postage stamp,** it was difficult to send a letter to another country. The sender paid for the letter to travel in his or her own country. Then the person in the other country paid for that part of the trip. If a letter **crossed** several countries, the problem was worse.

went across

Rowland Hill, a British teacher, had the idea of a postage stamp with **glue** on the back. The British post office made the first stamps in 1840. They were the Penny Black and the Twopence Blue. A person bought a stamp and put it on a letter. The post office **delivered** the letter. When people **received** letters, they didn't have to pay anything. The letters were **prepaid.**

took it to the person

got

paid for before

Postage stamps became popular in Great Britain **immediately.** Other countries started making their own postage stamps very quickly.

right away, right now

There were still problems with international **mail.** Some countries did not want to **accept** letters with stamps from another country. Finally, in 1874, a German organized the Universal Postal System. Each country in the UPS agreed to accept letters with prepaid postage from the other **members.** Today, the offices of the UPS are in Switzerland. Almost every country in the world is a member of this organization. It takes care of any international mail problems.

take

30 Today, post offices in every country sell beautiful stamps. Collecting stamps is one of the most popular hobbies in the world, and every stamp collector knows about the Penny Black and the Twopence Blue.

◾A◾ Vocabulary

Put the right word in the blanks. The sentences are from the text.

crossed	received	postage	glue
prepaid	members	international	mail
stamp	delivered	immediately	accept

1. When people _____ letters, they didn't have to pay anything.
2. Before the invention of the _____ _____, it was difficult to send a letter to another country.
3. The post office _____ the letter.
4. Each country in the UPS agreed to accept letters with prepaid postage from the other _____ _____.
5. If a letter _____ several countries, the problem was worse.
6. Postage stamps became popular in Great Britain _____.
7. Some countries did not want to _____ letters with stamps from other countries.
8. The letters were _____.
9. There were still problems with international _____ ____.
10. Rowland Hill, a British teacher, had the idea of a postage stamp with _____ on the back.

◾B◾ Vocabulary (new context)

Put the right word in the blanks.

prepay	cross	postage	members
deliver	worse	mail	immediately
accept	stamps	glue	receive

1. Jamal and Marie are _____ of the International Students Club.

2. When you rent an apartment for a year, you have to _____ the last month's rent. You pay the first and the last month's rent.

3. Children have to be careful when they _____ the street.

4. Mr. Ross is going to the post office because he has to buy some _____.

5. If you buy living room furniture, the store will _____ it to your house.

6. How much is the _____ for an airmail letter to Japan?

7. Did you _____ any letters this week?

8. Please go to your office _____. You have a phone call.

9. The teacher will not _____ homework if it is a week late. She won't take it.

10. Did you get any _____ today?

11. _____ helps a stamp stay on a letter.

C Vocabulary Review: Opposites

Match the words that mean the opposite.

Column A
1. apart _____
2. bought _____
3. found _____
4. arrived _____
5. bottom _____
6. know _____
7. glad _____
8. unusual _____
9. able _____
10. birth _____
11. saved _____
12. at first _____
13. brave _____
14. left _____

Column B

a. top
b. left
c. suppose
d. spent
e. took
f. unable
g. gold
h. choose

i. finally
j. afraid
k. together
l. death
m. ordinary
n. sold
o. unhappy
p. lost

D Comprehension: True/False/No Information

Write T if the sentence is true. Write F if it is false. Write NI if there is no information given.

———— 1. Before postage stamps, two people paid for letters to travel in two countries.
———— 2. A teacher invented the postage stamp.
———— 3. He was American.
———— 4. The first two stamps were colored black and blue.
———— 5. A stamp shows that the postage is prepaid.
———— 6. The United States was the second country to make postage stamps.
———— 7. Postage stamps solved all mail problems immediately.
———— 8. Members of the UPS accept prepaid letters from other countries.
———— 9. Kuwait is a member of the UPS.
———— 10. All the UPS officials are Swiss.
———— 11. Stamp collecting is a popular hobby.

E Questions

The asterisk (*) means you have to think of the answer. You cannot find it in the text.

1. Why was it difficult to send a letter to another country before the invention of the postage stamp?
2. Who invented the postage stamp?
3. When did he invent it?
4. What country was he from?
5. Were postage stamps popular?
*6. Why were they popular?
7. What does *prepaid* mean?
*8. Why didn't countries want to accept mail with stamps from other countries?
9. What does the Universal Postal System do today?
10. Where are its offices?
*11. Why do people like to collect stamps?
*12. Why do stamp collectors know about the Penny Black?

F Main Idea

Which is the main idea of this chapter? Choose one.

1. Rowland Hill, a British teacher, invented the postage stamp.
2. When Mr. Hill invented the postage stamp, it solved a lot of problems.
3. People collect stamps because every country makes beautiful ones.

Pencils and Pens

LESSON

3

Pre-reading Questions

1. Who in the class has a pen? A pencil?
2. Do you do your homework in pen or in pencil? Why?
3. How do people sharpen pencils?

3

Pencils and Pens

No one knows who invented pencils or when it happened. A Swiss described a pencil in a book in 1565. He said it was a piece of wood with **lead** inside it. (Lead is a very heavy
5 metal.) Pencils weren't popular, and people continued to write with pens. They used bird feathers as pens.

Then in 1795 someone started making pencils from **graphite** and they became very
10 popular. Graphite is a kind of **coal.** (Coal is black, and we burn it for heat and energy.) Today people make pencils in the same way. They **grind** the graphite, make it into the shape of a stick, and bake it. Then they put it
15 inside a piece of wood. One pencil can write 50,000 English words or make a line 55 kilometers long.

People wrote with feather pens and then used pens with metal **points.** They had to **dip**
20 the point into **ink** after every few letters. Next someone invented a **fountain pen** that could hold ink inside it. A fountain pen can write several pages before you have to fill it again.

Two Hungarian brothers, Ladislao and
25 Georg Biro, invented the **ballpoint** pen that we all use today. They left Hungary and started making ballpoint pens in England in 1943 during World War II. English **pilots** liked the pens. They

fountain pen

drivers of airplanes

couldn't write with fountain pens in airplanes
30 because the ink **leaked** out. Later, a French company called Bic bought the Biro's company.

Some people call ballpoint pens a bic.
Australians call them biros. **Whatever** we call
them, we use them every day.

leaked

anything

A Vocabulary

Put the right word in the blanks. The sentences are from the text.

ballpoint	points	graphite	lead
coal	dip	whatever	leaked
grind	pilots	ink	fountain pen

1. They couldn't write with fountain pens in airplanes because the ink
   _____ out.
2. Then in 1795 someone started making pencils from _____
   and they became very popular.
3. He said it was a piece of wood with _____ inside it.
4. People wrote with feather pens and then used pens with metal
   _____.
5. Graphite is a kind of _____.
6. Next someone invented a _____ that could hold ink inside it.
7. They had to _____ the point into _____
   after every few letters.
8. They _____ the graphite, make it into the shape of a
   stick, and bake it.
9. Two Hungarian brothers, Ladislao and Georg Biro, invented the
   _____ pen that we all use today.
10. _____ we call them, we use them every day.

B Vocabulary (new context)

Put the right word in the blanks.

graphite	ballpoint	pilot	lead
coal	leaks	grind	fountain pen
ink	point	dips	whatever

1. Our shower _____. A little water runs out of it all day.
2. Dead plants and animals became _____ and petroleum millions of years ago.
3. You should have a good _____ on your pencil.
4. Yoko's brother is a _____. He flies for Japan Airlines.
5. _____ is a soft, heavy metal.
6. Students a hundred years ago always had a bottle of _____ on their desk.
7. Dan works in an ice cream store. He _____ out ice cream for people.
8. We _____ coffee before we mix it with hot water.
9. Most people use _____ pens, but some people like a _____ _____.
10. At a cafeteria, you can choose _____ you want to eat.

■C■ Vocabulary Review

Put the right word in the blanks.

by herself	team	lucky	listened
size	apart	slide	embarrassed
strip	bend	row	fastener
dozen	hook	flexible	axe

1. There are about a _____ students in the class. It is a small class.
2. Mountain climbers always carry a little _____ with them.
3. What _____ cola do you want, small or large?
4. People often _____ over when they talk to children.
5. A children's park always has a _____. Children can _____ down it.
6. My little daughter is pleased that she can get dressed _____ now.
7. Masako was _____ when she gave the wrong answer in class.
8. How many people are on a soccer _____?
9. Robert took his bicycle _____ and now he can't put it back together again.

10. There is a _____ on the back of the door. You can hang your jacket there.

11. Jean-Paul _____ to classical music when he went home last night.

12. Maria always sits in the front _____ of the class.

D Comprehension

Put a circle around the letter of the best answer. The asterisk (*) means you have to think of the answer. You cannot find it in the text.

1. _____ described a pencil in 1565.
   a. A Hungarian   c. A Frenchman
   b. A Swiss   d. An Englishman

2. The first pencils had _____ in them.
   a. gold   c. lead
   b. graphite   d. ink

3. One pencil can write _____ words.
   a. 50,000   c. 55
   b. 55,000   d. 1565

4. The first pens were _____.
   a. wooden   c. metal
   b. feathers   d. graphite

5. The next pens had a _____ point.
   a. wooden   c. metal
   b. lead   d. silver

6. A fountain pen can hold _____ inside it.
   a. coal   c. graphite
   b. lead   d. ink

7. The Biro brothers made thousands of pens in _____.
   a. England   c. France
   b. Hungary   d. Switzerland

8. _____ are best for writing in airplanes.
    a. Ballpoint pens   c. Fountain pens
    b. Pencils   d. a and b

*9. People burn _____.
    a. coal and graphite   c. coal and wood
    b. graphite and lead   d. lead and coal

*10. People grind _____.
    a. hamburger meat   c. graphite
    b. coffee   d. a, b, and c

E Questions

The asterisk (*) means you have to think of the answer. You cannot find it in the text.

1. Who invented the pencil? When?
2. Describe the pencils in 1565.
3. Describe a modern pencil.
4. How do people make pencils today?
5. What kind of pens did people write with after feather pens?
6. Why was a fountain pen better than the old pens?
7. Where were the inventors of the ballpoint pen from?
8. Why is a ballpoint better than a fountain pen for pilots?
*9. Why does a fountain pen leak in an airplane?
10. In what country are Bic pens made?
11. Where did the name *biro* come from?
*12. Which is better, a pencil or a ballpoint pen?

F Main Idea

Which is the main idea of this chapter? Choose one.

1. There were several kinds of pens before ballpoint pens.
2. We use pens and pencils every day.
3. Ballpoint pens and pencils are very useful inventions.

Umbrellas

Pre-reading Questions

LESSON

4

1. Do you have an umbrella? How often do you use it?

2. Some people say not to open an umbrella in the house. They say it is bad luck. Do you believe that?

3. What do you do when it rains and you do not have an umbrella?

Umbrellas

The umbrella is a very ordinary **object.** It keeps the rain and the sun off people. Most umbrellas **fold up,** so it is easy to carry them.

thing

However, the umbrella did not begin life as
5 an ordinary object. It was a sign of **royalty** or importance. Some African **tribes** still use umbrellas in this way today. Someone carries an umbrella and walks behind the king or important person.

kings, queens, and their families

Umbrellas are very old. The Chinese had
10 them in the eleventh century B.C. From there, umbrellas traveled to India, Persia, and Egypt. In Greece and Rome, men **wouldn't** use them. They believed umbrellas were only for women.

past of won't

When the Spanish explorers went to Mexico,
15 they saw the Aztec kings using umbrellas. English explorers saw Native American **princes** carrying umbrellas on the east coast of North America. It **seems** that people in different parts of the world invented umbrellas at different times.

sons of queens and kings

20 England was probably the first country in Europe where ordinary people used umbrellas against the rain. England has a rainy **climate,** and umbrellas are very useful there.

Everybody uses umbrellas today. The next
25 time you carry one, remember that for centuries only great men and women used them. Perhaps you are really a king or queen, a **princess** or prince.

daughter of a king and queen

A Vocabulary

Put the right word in the blanks. The sentences are from the text.

wouldn't queens princes princess
king object climate tribes
royalty importance fold up seems

1. English explorers saw Native American _____ carrying umbrellas on the east coast of North America.
2. It was a sign of _____ or importance.
3. England has a rainy _____, and umbrellas are very useful there.
4. The umbrella is a very ordinary _____.
5. In Greece and Rome, men _____ use them.
6. Perhaps you are really a king or queen, a _____ or prince.
7. Some African _____ still use umbrellas in this way today.
8. Most umbrellas _____, so it is easy to carry them.
9. It _____ that people in different parts of the world invented umbrellas at different times.

B Vocabulary (new context)

Put the right word in the blanks.

prince princess objects seems
importance fold wouldn't climate
queen king royalty tribe

1. A _____ is the daughter of a king and queen. A _____ is the son of a king and queen. They are all _____.

2. Bill _____ very unhappy today. What is wrong?
3. The Yanomami had no metal. They only had _____ made of wood and stone.
4. Dan asked Maria to go to the movies with him last night, but she _____ go. She was too tired.
5. The Hopi are a _____ in Arizona.
6. Qatar has a desert _____, but Malaysia is in the tropics.

7. After you write a letter, you _____ it and put it in an envelope.

C Vocabulary Review

Underline the word that does not belong.

1. around, about, nearly, behind
2. movie theater, art museum, gymnasium, science museum
3. governor, collector, traveler, sailor
4. jungle, navy, forest, trees
5. game, team, win, adventure
6. dozen, eighteen, kilo, eleven
7. hook, button, flexible, zipper
8. slide, receive, take, accept
9. lead, gold, coal, silver
10. princes, kings, queens, princess

D Comprehension

Put a circle around the letter of the best answer. The asterisk (*) means you have to think of the answer. You cannot find it in the text.

1. Today, people use umbrellas for _____.
   a. the rain
   b. the sun
   c. a sign of a great person
   d. a, b, and c

2. A queen is a _____ person.
   a. royal
   b. embarrassing
   c. holiday
   d. jewelry

3. A great person walks _____ someone with an umbrella.
   a. beside
   b. before
   c. in front of
   d. in back of

4. India and Persia learned about umbrellas from _____.
   a. Aztecs
   b. Egypt
   c. China
   d. Spanish explorers

*5. Most groups of people had some kind of _____.
   a. coal   c. ink
   b. royalty   d. mail

6. Native Americans _____.
   a. learned about umbrellas from English and Spanish explorers
   b. invented umbrellas
   c. got umbrellas from the Chinese
   d. taught Egyptians about umbrellas

7. English people started using umbrellas because they have _____.
   a. royalty   c. too much sun
   b. a rainy climate   d. great men and women

E Questions

The asterisk (*) means you have to think of the answer. You cannot find it in the text.

1. What are two uses of an umbrella?
*2. Why is it easier to carry an umbrella that folds up?
3. What was an umbrella a sign of in the past?
4. Who uses umbrellas in this way today?
*5. How do we know that the Chinese had umbrellas in the eleventh century B.C.?
6. Why didn't Greek men use umbrellas?
7. What other people invented the umbrella?
8. Why did English people like umbrellas?
*9. In what countries are umbrellas not very useful?

F Main Idea

Which is the main idea for this chapter? Choose one.

1. For centuries only great people used umbrellas, but now ordinary people everywhere use them.
2. Umbrellas are useful in the rain.
3. The Chinese and Native Americans invented umbrellas.

The Metric System

METRIC CHART

LENGTH
1000 millimeters = 1 meter
100 centimeters = 1 meter
1 kilometer = 1000 meters

AREA
100 square millimeters =
1 square centimeter
100 square meters = 1 are
100 ares = 1 hectare
100 hectares = 1 square kilometer

VOLUME
1000 milliliters = 1 liter
100 centiliters = 1 liter
10 deciliters = 1 liter
1 kiloliter = 1000 liters

WEIGHT
1000 milligrams = 1 gram
100 centigrams = 1 gram
1 kilogram = 1000 grams
1 metric ton = 1000 kilograms

LESSON

Pre-reading Questions

1. Does your country use the metric system?
2. Do you know another system of measurement?
3. Which countries do not use the metric system?

The Metric System

People all over the world use kilograms, centimeters, square meters, liters, and Celsius (C). These are all ways to **measure** things. They are all part of the **metric system.**

5   During the French **Revolution** (1789–1799) against the king, the revolutionary government started the metric system. Before that, every part of France had a different system for measuring things. Also, cloth makers measured

10   cloth with one system. Jewelers used another system. Carpenters used another. Other countries used other systems. The revolutionary government wanted one international scientific system of measurement. They asked a group of scientists

15   and mathematicians to invent a system.

The mathematicians and scientists **decided** to use the numbers ten, hundred, and thousand for their system.

Next they had to decide on a "natural"

20   **length.** They chose one ten-millionth (1/10,000,000) of the **distance** from the **Equator** to the North Pole. They called this one meter. Then they chose one gram for weighing things. A **cubic** centimeter of water

25   weighs one gram.

Mathematicians and scientists worked on these problems for twenty years until they finally finished the complete system. The biggest problem was measuring the meter.

war by the people against their government

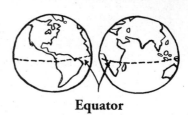

Equator

noun for *long*

distance = how far

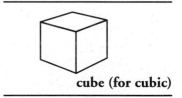

cube (for cubic)

30   The metric system was a wonderful gift to the world. There are only a few countries that don't use it. The United States is one. The metric system is truly an international system.

A Vocabulary

Put the right word in the blanks. The sentences are from the text.

Revolution	ten-millionth	Equator	cubic	Celsius	length
centimeters	decided	system	metric	measure	distance

1. During the French _____ (1789–1799) against the king, the revolutionary government started the metric system.
2. Next they had to decide on a "natural" _____.
3. They are all part of the _____ _____.
4. A _____ centimeter of water weighs one gram.
5. They chose one ten-millionth of the _____ from the _____ to the North Pole.
6. These are all ways to _____ things.
7. The mathematicians and scientists _____ to use the numbers ten, hundred, and thousand for their system.

B Vocabulary (new context)

Put the right word in the blanks.

liter	distance	system	Equator	decided	metric
square	Revolution	measure	length	cube	gram

1. The Russian _____ in 1917 was against the royal family of Russia.
2. What is the _____ between Chicago and New York?
3. The _____ system is a system of measurement.
4. Junko Tabei, a Japanese housewife, _____ to try to climb Mount Everest.
5. We need to buy a tablecloth. Please _____ the table so we will know what size to buy. What is the _____ of the table? How long is it?
6. Indonesia, Kenya, and the Amazon area are all on the _____.

7. A _____ has six sides. Each side is the same size.
8. The British had the first _____ of prepaid postage.

C   Vocabulary Review

Put the right word in the blanks.

lonely	evaporated	percent	basket
broom	section	tires	crossed
postage	deliver	prepaid	stamp
immediately	member	point	jazz

1. Keiko doesn't like to be away from her family. She feels _____.
2. Beef is in the meat _____ of a supermarket.
3. Ninety-five _____ of the class passed the test.
4. Letters that go outside a country take more _____ than letters inside a country.
5. Alice came in from the garden with a _____ of beautiful flowers.
6. Did the mail carrier _____ the mail yet?
7. The _____ on my pencil is broken. May I sharpen it?
8. Some people do not like to listen to _____.
9. There is no water left in the dish. It all _____.
10. We need two new front _____ for the car.
11. The Polynesians _____ the Pacific Ocean in double canoes.
12. Carl is a _____ of the stamp club. Collecting stamps is his hobby.

D   Comprehension: True/False/No Information

Write T if the sentence is true. Write F if it is false. Write NI if there is no information given.

_____ 1. Celsius is part of the metric system.
_____ 2. Hectares are part of the metric system.
_____ 3. We use the metric system to measure things.
_____ 4. The French Revolution was in the seventeenth century.
_____ 5. The metric system is an international scientific system of measurement.
_____ 6. A mathematician and a scientist invented the metric system.
_____ 7. France gave the world a wonderful gift.

_____ 8. The United States uses the metric system.

_____ 9. The United States uses an old English system of measurement.

_____ 10. The French Revolution was after the American Revolution.

E Questions

The asterisk (*) means you have to think of the answer. You cannot find it in the text.

*1. What do *centi-* and *milli-* mean?
2. What is the metric system?
3. Who was the French Revolution against?
4. Before the Revolution, there was a problem in France about measuring things. What was it?
5. Who invented the metric system?
6. What did they choose for the "natural" length?
7. How did they choose one gram?
8. How long did it take to complete the system?
9. Why do we call this an international system of measurement?
*10. Why is the metric system easy to use?

F Main Idea

Put the number of the details after the main ideas. Some details go with more than one main idea.

1. **The Zipper**
2. **The Postage Stamp**
3. **The Pencil**

4. **The Ballpoint Pen**
5. **The Umbrella**
6. **The Metric System**

a. A British teacher invented it.
b. French scientists and mathematicians invented it.
c. Different groups of people invented it.
d. An American invented it.
e. No one knows who invented it.
f. Two Hungarian brothers invented it.
g. It is international and scientific.

h. Sometimes it is a sign of royalty.
i. The United States doesn't use it.
j. It is a fastener.
k. One of them can write 50,000 words.
l. It is better than a fountain pen in an airplane.
m. People in many countries use it.
n. Collecting them is a popular hobby.

Word Study

A   Will/Be + going to

There are two ways to write about the future in English.

1. **Will + simple verb**

Example: Carol **will lend** me her car tomorrow.

Classes **will end** next week.

2. **Be (am, is, are) + going to + simple verb**

Example: The store **is going to deliver** our new refrigerator this afternoon.

I **am going to measure** the kitchen floor.

1. Write sentences with *will* and the word in parentheses.

Example: travel (next summer)

My parents will travel in Japan for two months next summer.

a.   receive (next week)
b.   deliver (tomorrow)
c.   decide (tonight)
d.   arrive (tomorrow morning)
e.   go skiing (next winter)

2. Write sentences with *be going to* and the words in parentheses.

Example: attend (next week)

I am going to attend my cousin's wedding next week.

a.   continue (next fall)
b.   practice (all summer)
c.   choose (tomorrow)
d.   roast (tonight)
e.   leave (next month)

B How + Adjective

Examples: **How far** is it to Los Angeles?
How old are you?
How large is your country?
How heavy is a hippopotamus?

Use these words in questions.

1. how long
2. how deep
3. how tall

4. how much
5. how fast

C Irregular Verbs

1. **Learn these verb forms. Then use each past form in a sentence.**

	Simple	Past		Simple	Past
a.	keep	kept	f.	freeze	froze
b.	hurt	hurt	g.	lose	lost
c.	lead	led	h.	pay	paid
d.	write	wrote	i.	speak	spoke
e.	wear	wore	j.	build	built

2. **Write the past of these verbs.**

a. blow _____
b. give _____
c. know _____
d. shop _____
e. meet _____
f. understand _____

g. choose _____
h. grow _____
i. leave _____
j. hit _____
k. fall _____
l. send _____

D Word Forms

	Verb	Noun	Adjective
1.	collect	collection collector	
2.	describe	description	descriptive
3.	heat	heat	hot
4.		royalty	royal

Verb	Noun	Adjective
5.	importance	important
6. pollute	pollution	polluted
7. believe	belief	believable
8. rain	rain	rainy
9. sharpen	sharpener	sharp
10. measure	measurement	measurable

Put the right word form in the blanks. Use a word from Line 1 for Sentence 1 and so on. Use the right form of the verb and singular and plural nouns.

1. Lois is a stamp _____. She _____ stamps. She has a large _____.
2. Write a _____ of your city. _____ it.
3. We need some _____ water. Please _____ some.
4. Prince Charles is a member of the British _____ family. His parents are _____ too.
5. In India umbrellas were a sign of _____. Only _____ people used them.
6. Toxic substances are a form of _____. They can _____ the air and the water. Then the environment is _____.
7. Many people _____ that God made the earth. This is their _____.
8. It is starting to _____. We are going to have a _____ day. Do you like the _____?
9. Where is the pencil _____? My pencil isn't _____. I need to _____ it.
10. Please _____ the size of the living room carpet. How long and how wide is it? What are the _____?

E Writing

Choose one or more of these topics and write answers.

1. Which inventions in *Unit I* are the most important in your own life? Why?
2. Can you think of a new invention? Describe it.
3. Think of a very important invention in your country. Describe it.

Video Highlights

A Before You Watch

1. How many of the famous people in this chart do you know about? Work with a small group to fill in the chart. You do not need to use complete sentences.

Famous People	Facts about them
Elvis Presley	*Rock-n-roll singer, lived in the U.S.*
Marilyn Monroe	
Ronald Reagan	
Sylvester Stallone	
John Lennon	
Barbra Streisand	
Pope John Paul	

2. Have you seen these people on stamps? What other famous people have you seen on a stamp?

B As You Watch

1. Check the countries that you hear in the video.

_____ Canada	_____ Nicaragua
_____ Uganda	_____ Honduras
_____ Switzerland	_____ Cameroon
_____ China	_____ Liberia
_____ The U.S.A.	_____ Ghana
_____ Mexico	_____ St. Vincent and the Grenadines

2. Complete the description of this stamp. Use the names of places in the list below.

Liberia	London	Paris	China
Hong Kong	New York	Zambia	Canada

This stamp was made to celebrate the transition of _____ to the Chinese. The company that designed this stamp is in _____. The factory that produces this stamp is in _____. The people who use this stamp live in _____ and _____.

©CNN

C After You Watch

1. Look at the map and find two of the countries from the lists above. Circle the countries.

2. Read the information about the postal system in one of these countries and answer the questions that follow.

Dominica
Martinique
Caribbean Sea
St. Lucia
St. Vincent and the Grenadines
Barbados
Grenada
Trinidad & Tobago

Grenada is a small island in the Caribbean Sea. Its population is about 104,000, and its official language is English. Grenada is a member of the Universal Postal System, so Grenadians can send and receive international mail. However, no one in the country has the equipment necessary to produce stamps.

The Philatela Company in New York City produces stamps for more than seventy countries. Like Grenada, most of these countries do not make their own stamps. They must buy them from another place. Many of the stamps that the Grenadian postal system buys from Philatela have beautiful pictures of famous people on them. The company artists design the stamps and the post office officials decide if they like them or not. Sometimes, new stamps are so interesting that collectors want to buy them, too.

Put T if the sentence is true. Put F if it is false. Put NI if no information is given.

_____ a. Grenadians speak English.
_____ b. Many Grenadians write letters.
_____ c. Grenada produces its own stamps.
_____ d. The artists at Philatela design many stamps with famous people on them
_____ e. There are many stamp collectors in Grenada.

Activity Page

Across

1. The post office _____ letters and packages
3. A _____ is strong, but it opens and closes easily
4. _____ Hill, a British teacher, had the idea of putting glue on the back of a postage stamp.
5. My pen is out of _____.
6. The strips of cloth are flexible. They _____ easily.

Down

1. You have to _____ a fountain pen in ink.
2. Every letter needs one of these.
7. She still _____ me $10.
8. Paid for in advance.
9. Same as #1 down.
10. There are five students in each _____.

35

Dictionary Page

Finding Antonyms

Antonyms are words that have opposite meanings. For example, the antonym of *hot* is *cold*.

When you look up a word in your dictionary, you can often find its antonym at the end of the definition.

> **accept** /ık'sɛpt/ *verb*
> **1**   to take willingly: *He accepted my apology for being late.*
> **2**   to say "yes," that you will do something: *Are you going to accept his invitation to the party? (antonym)* refuse

A. Write the antonyms for each of these words. Use your dictionary to check your answers.

apart   _____

easy   _____

hate   _____

high   _____

receive   _____

rigid   _____

slowly   _____

wide   _____

B. Now use one of the antonyms in each of the following sentences.

1. These shoes are wonderful for sports because they are both strong and _____.

2. We couldn't get the sofa into the room because the door was too
   _____.

3. It's great to have the whole family _____.

4. She couldn't answer the question. It was much too
   _____.

5. Monique walks very _____. I can't keep up with her.

Unusual Sports

Context Clues

Put a circle around the answer that means the same as the word or words in **bold.**

1. It is very cold in Norway in winter. You have to wear a heavy coat, a hat on your head, and **gloves** on your hands.
   a. something to keep the hands warm
   b. something to make the hands look pretty
   c. something to cool the hands
   d. something that makes the hands work better

2. People cannot ride their bicycles on the **sidewalk** because it is dangerous for the people walking there. They have to ride in the street.
   a. the middle of the street
   b. a place at the side of the street for people to walk
   c. a beautiful part of a park
   d. a place for cars and motorcycles

3. Mr. da Silva's little boy was going to run into the street. Mr. da Silva **yelled** at him to come back.
   a. pushed quickly
   b. put out
   c. seemed
   d. spoke loudly

4. A hundred years ago people crossed the ocean by ship. This was slow. Today we travel by plane at a **high speed.**
   a. slowly
   b. independently
   c. very fast
   d. luckily

5. Captain Lee **trains** new police officers. The new officers study and practice for their new jobs.
   a. belongs to
   b. teaches
   c. agrees
   d. shaves

6. In a basketball game, one player **passes** the ball to another player.
   a. sends
   b. decides
   c. takes
   d. throws

7. Oman is one of the Arab **nations.**
   a. countries
   b. religions
   c. mountains
   d. governors

8. Barbara had her coffee cup in front of her. When she finished drinking her coffee, she pushed the cup **aside.**
   a. off the table
   b. to the side
   c. into the kitchen
   d. into the air

9. Carol visited all the capital cities in Europe **except** Rome. She didn't have time to go there.
   a. when
   b. so
   c. but
   d. that

10. I'm sorry we can't talk any longer, but we are going to be late. We have to **rush.**
    a. hurry
    b. lead
    c. carry
    d. grow

11. Switzerland has beautiful high mountains. However, people can't live high in the mountains because life there is too difficult. They live in the **valleys.**
    a. large cities on grasslands
    b. tropical forests
    c. low areas between mountains
    d. hot desert areas

12. Today is my younger brother's school sports day. There are games all morning. In the afternoon he is going to run in a foot **race.**
    a. volleyball game
    b. running competition
    c. competition among horses
    d. skiing competition

13. Running is usually an **individual** sport. Volleyball and basketball are team sports.
    a. group of people
    b. team
    c. several people together
    d. one person

14. Pierre wrote an **excellent** composition. It is the best one in the class.
    a. very, very good
    b. not interesting
    c. poor
    d. boring

15. The teacher walked **ahead** of the students. He was leading the way to the new classroom.
    a. in back of
    b. near
    c. beside
    d. in front of

16. Coke and Pepsi are **similar** drinks. Seven-Up tastes different.
    a. different
    b. almost the same
    c. fried
    d. dark

Thai Boxing

LESSON

1

Pre-reading Questions

1. Does your country have this sport?

2. Can a person always use his elbows and knees in boxing?

3. Do you think boxing is dangerous?

Thai Boxing

Boxing is popular in many countries. Two fighters wear boxing **gloves** on their hands. A bell rings. The boxers hit each other until one **knocks out** the other. Each part of the fight is three minutes long. It is called a **round.**

Thai boxing is different.

The boxing **match** begins with music from **drums** and **flutes.** Then the two fighters **kneel** and **pray** to God. Next they do a slow dance that copies the movements of Thai boxing. During this dance, each fighter tries to show the other that he is best.

Then the fight begins. In Thai boxing, the fighters can **kick** with their feet and hit each other with their **elbows** and knees. Of course, they hit with their hands too. Each round is three minutes long. Then the boxers have a two-minute rest. Most boxers can fight only five rounds because this kind of fighting is very difficult.

Thai boxing began over five hundred (500) years ago. If a soldier lost his **weapons** in a **battle**, he needed to fight with just his body. The soldiers learned how to use all the parts of their body. In 1560, the Burmese army **captured** Naresuen, the King of Thailand, in a war. King Naresuen was a very good boxer. He won his **freedom** from Burma by defeating all the best Burmese fighters. When he returned to Thailand, his people were very **proud** of him. Thai boxing became a popular sport.

gloves

competition

bend down on the knees

drum

hit with the feet

the part of the arm that bends

flute

battle = a fight

weapons

A Vocabulary

Put the right word in the blanks. The sentences are from the text.

gloves	match	kick	proud
round	weapons	captured	knocks out
kneel	elbows	battle	freedom
copies	pray	flutes	drums

1. The boxers hit each other until one _____ the other.
2. The boxing _____ begins with music from _____ and _____.
3. In Thai boxing, the fighters can _____ with their feet and hit each other with their _____ and knees.
4. Two fighters wear boxing _____ on their hands.
5. If a soldier lost his _____ in a _____, he needed to fight with just his body.
6. He won his _____ from Burma by defeating all the best Burmese fighters.
7. It is called a _____.
8. Then the two fighters _____ and _____ to God.
9. In 1560, the Burmese army _____ Naresuen, the King of Thailand, in a war.
10. When he returned to Thailand, his people were very _____ of him.

B Vocabulary (new context)

Put the right word in the blanks.

match	copies	kneel	weapons
freedom	drums	flutes	knock
captured	pray	elbows	boxers
gloves	kick	battles	proud

1. It is cold today. You should wear _____ and a hat.
2. Many people of the world make music with _____ and _____.
3. There is a tennis _____ on television tomorrow afternoon.
4. You have to _____ down when you pick up something on the floor.

5. The scientists _____ a dolphin so they could study it.
6. Your knees are part of your legs. Your _____ are part of your arms.
7. Religious people _____ every day.
8. Nadia got a good grade on her quiz. She is _____ of herself.
9. In soccer you can _____ the ball. In basketball you can throw it.
10. Most countries in the world spend too much money on _____ for the army.
11. There are terrible _____ in a war.
12. Kenya was a British colony. It won its _____ in 1953.

C Vocabulary Review

Match the words that mean the same.

Column A
1. composer _____
2. caffeine _____
3. object _____
4. distance _____
5. revolution _____
6. Equator _____
7. whatever _____
8. princess _____
9. independent _____
10. over _____
11. blues _____
12. prince _____
13. climate _____

Column B
a. a kind of music
b. anything
c. the sister of a prince
d. the brother of a princess
e. music writer
f. war
g. finished
h. free
i. something in coffee and tea
j. weather
k. dip
l. thing
m. how far
n. leak
o. line around the middle of the earth

D Comprehension

Put a circle around the letter of the best answer.

1. Most boxing begins with a _____.
   a. bell   b. drum   c. flute   d. b and c

2. Thai boxers don't hit with their _____.
   a. hands   b. elbows   c. knees   d. heads

3. Thai boxers _____ before the fight.
   a. grind   b. knock out   c. pray   d. capture

4. They pray on their _____.
   a. elbows   b. backs   c. hands   d. knees

5. Thai boxing began _____.
   a. as a sport   b. in the navy   c. in the army   d. as a dance

6. _____ made Thai boxing a popular sport.
   a. A Burmese   b. A king   c. A soldier   d. The army

7. The king's people were _____.
   a. proud of him   b. royalty   c. defeated   d. captured

E   Questions

The asterisk (*) means you have to think of the answer. You cannot find it in the text.

1. What do boxers wear on their hands?
2. What is one part of a fight called?
3. How does a Thai boxing match begin?
4. What do the boxers do before they start fighting?
5. Why do they do a slow dance?
6. How is Thai boxing different from other boxing?
7. What is the length of a round in Thai boxing?
8. Why did Thai soldiers learn to box?
9. How did King Naresuen win his freedom?
10. How did his people feel about this?
*11. Is boxing safe or dangerous? Why?
*12. Is Thai boxing safer or more dangerous than other boxing? Why?

F   Main Idea

Which is the main idea of this chapter? Choose one.

1. Thai boxing has music before the match.
2. Most Thai boxers can fight only a short time.
3. Thai boxing is different from other boxing.

Curling

LESSON

2

Pre-reading Questions

1. Why do the people in the picture have brooms?

2. Why do you think there are circles of different sizes on the ice?

3. What do you think the handles on the stone are for?

2

Curling

Curling is a popular sport in Canada. However, it probably started in Scotland or Holland around three hundred (300) years ago.

⁵ There are two teams with four people on each team in curling. They play on a sheet of ice that is 45 meters long and 4.3 meters wide.

Each player slides two heavy stones toward the "house" circle at the opposite end of the ice

¹⁰ sheet. The stones weigh almost twenty kilos. Each stone is **flat** on the top and bottom and has a **handle** on the top. The player uses the handle to slide the stone. The player **swings** the stone off the ice, and it curls or **curves** as it

¹⁵ slides along. It does not go in a **straight** line.

While one player throws the stone, his teammates sweep in front of the stone. This **smoothes** the ice. The players believe that the stone travels faster on smooth ice, and it can

²⁰ go farther. The **captain** of the team **yells**, "Sweep!" and the teammates start sweeping the ice.

Usually people sweep the floor or the **sidewalk** with a broom. They don't sweep as a

²⁵ sport. Curling is an unusual game.

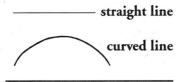

—————— **straight line**

curved line

captain = leader/yells = says loudly

A Vocabulary

Put the right word in the blanks. The sentences are from the text.

sweep	teammates	handle	curling
yells	smoothes	flat	sidewalk
straight	swings	captain	curves

1. _____ is a popular sport in Canada.
2. The player _____ the stone off the ice and it curls or _____ as it slides along.
3. Usually people sweep the floor or the _____ with a broom.
4. Each stone is _____ on the top and bottom and has a _____ on the top.
5. It does not go in a _____ line.
6. The _____ of the team _____ "Sweep!" and the teammates start sweeping the ice.
7. This _____ the ice.

B Vocabulary (new context)

Put the right word in the blanks.

curly	straight	sweep	yelled
sidewalk	teammates	captain	flat
handle	smooth	swing	curves

1. When Gary saw his friend down the street, he _____ to him.
2. Pam's hair is wavy, Ruth's hair is _____, and Keiko's hair is _____.
3. Paper is _____.
4. Mrs. White is going to cut the grass and sweep the _____ in front of her house.
5. Children like to _____ in the swings at our park.
6. A suitcase has a _____ on it. This makes it easy to carry.
7. You must drive carefully when there are a lot of _____ in the road.

8. Every ship has a _____ .
9. The top of a desk or table is _____ .

C Vocabulary Review

Put the right word in the blanks.

already	factory	guitar	either
footprints	pilot	seems	would
folded	tribe	system	decide
cubes	metric	kicked	gloves

1. My company plans to build a new _____ .
2. What is the temperature? It _____ cold today.
3. You can write with _____ a ballpoint pen or a pencil.
4. There were wet _____ on the floor near the shower.
5. The dancers _____ their feet into the air.
6. The _____ sounds lovely.
7. Each Arab _____ has its own name.
8. Glen _____ his clothes after he took them out of the dryer.
9. Bob can't _____ what to cook for dinner. He doesn't know what to cook.
10. _____ you like to go out to dinner tonight?
11. Some people buy sugar _____ for their coffee.
12. The _____ _____ uses meters and grams.

D Comprehension: True/False

Write T if the sentence is true. Write F if it is false. The asterisk (*) means you have to think of the answer. You cannot find it in the text.

_____ *1. Either the Scots or Dutch invented curling.
_____ *2. Canadians play curling all year round.
_____ 3. They play curling on a sheet of ice.
_____ 4. They play it with a ball.
_____ 5. The players throw small stones.
_____ *6. There are several sports where players slide stones on the ice.
_____ 7. Sweeping the ice makes it smooth.

_____ *8. The stones slide faster on smooth ice.
_____ 9. Team members sweep the ice to clean it.

E Questions

The asterisk (*) means you have to think of the answer. You cannot find it in the text.

1. Where is curling popular?
2. Did Canadians invent this game?
*3. How many people play curling at one time?
*4. Do Canadians play this game in summer?
5. How do the players slide the stones?
*6. Why is this game called curling?
7. Why do the players sweep the ice?
8. When does the captain of the team yell, "Sweep!"?

F Main Idea

Which is the main idea of this chapter? Choose one.

1. Canadians invented and play the unusual sport of curling.
2. Curling players sweep and slide stones on the ice.
3. Curling is an unusual game that Canadians play.

Lacrosse

LESSON

3

Pre-reading Questions

1. What other sports does this remind you of? Why?
2. Are the players wearing uniforms?
3. What do you think the aim of this sport is?

Lacrosse

Lacrosse is another popular sport in Canada. It is one of the oldest organized sports in America. The Native Americans in northern New York State and southern Ontario, Canada,
5 invented lacrosse. They used it to **train** for war. They invented this game before Columbus arrived in the New World.

practice

People play lacrosse outdoors. The **field** is seventy meters long. At each end of the field
10 there is a **goal**. The goal is a **net.** There are ten players on each team. Each player has a stick called a crosse. The players hit a ball that is 21 centimeters around and weighs 140 grams.

goal/net

They try to hit the ball into the net as many
15 times as possible. Lacrosse is a very fast game because the players can catch and **pass** the ball at a **high** **speed** with their sticks.

very fast

At one time lacrosse was the **national** summer sport in Canada. It is also popular in
20 Britain and Australia.

A Vocabulary

Put the right word in the blanks. The sentences are from the text.

arrived	national	train	high speed
oldest	seventy	goal	lacrosse
net	stick	field	pass

1. At one time lacrosse was the _____ summer sport in Canada.
2. At each end of the field there is a _____.
3. _____ is another popular sport in Canada.
4. Lacrosse is a very fast game because the players can catch and _____ the ball at a _____ with their sticks.
5. They used it to _____ for war.
6. The _____ is seventy meters long.
7. The goal is a _____.

B Vocabulary (new context)

Put the right word in the blanks.

training	goal	national	speed
passed	field	net	passed

1. The basketball player _____ the ball to his teammate. The teammate made a basket.
2. New firefighters get _____ in how to fight fires.
3. In volleyball, the teams hit the ball back and forth across the _____.
4. What is the _____ of light? How fast does light travel?
5. Each country has a _____ flag. The British, French, and American flags are red, white, and blue.
6. A soccer _____ has a _____ at each end.

C Vocabulary Review

Match the words that mean the same.

Column A
1. over _____
2. battle _____
3. dozen _____
4. wherever _____
5. match _____
6. object _____
7. accept _____
8. freedom _____
9. row _____
10. receive _____
11. pre- _____
12. adult _____

Column B
a. competition
b. independence
c. thing
d. before
e. take
f. flute
g. fighting
h. pray
i. finished
j. anywhere
k. line
l. twelve
m. get
n. grownup

D Comprehension

Choose the lettered answer that completes the sentence correctly. The asterisk (*) means you have to think of the answer. You cannot find it in the text.

1. Lacrosse was the national summer sport in _____.
   a. Canada
   b. England
   c. Australia
   d. New York State

2. _____ invented lacrosse.
   a. Columbus
   b. Native Americans
   c. Canadians
   d. A team

3. They invented lacrosse to _____ for war.
   a. fight
   b. pass
   c. train
   d. sweep

4. People play lacrosse _____.
   a. on a field
   b. in a stadium
   c. on a sheet of ice
   d. indoors

*5. _____ people play in a lacrosse game.
   a. Eight   c. Fifteen
   b. Twenty   d. Thirty

6. The players _____.
   a. hit a ball with a stick   c. swing and slide a stone
   b. hit each other   d. kick a ball

7. The players catch and pass the ball very _____.
   a. quickly   c. slowly
   b. heavily   d. yearly

*8. _____ is the national sport of the United States.
   a. Soccer   c. Basketball
   b. Boxing   d. Baseball

E Questions

The asterisk (*) means you have to think of the answer. You cannot find it in the text.

1. Who invented lacrosse?
*2. How is lacrosse like Thai boxing?
3. What countries play lacrosse?
4. How many goals are there?
5. How many players are on each team?
6. What does each player have?
7. What do the players try to do?
8. Why is lacrosse a fast game?
*9. Why don't they play lacrosse in winter in Canada?
*10. What is an organized sport?

F Main Idea

Which is the main idea of this chapter? Choose one.

1. The Native Americans invented lacrosse, a fast game that is popular in Canada.
2. Lacrosse is an outdoor game that is very fast.
3. In lacrosse, two teams use sticks to hit a ball.

Sumo

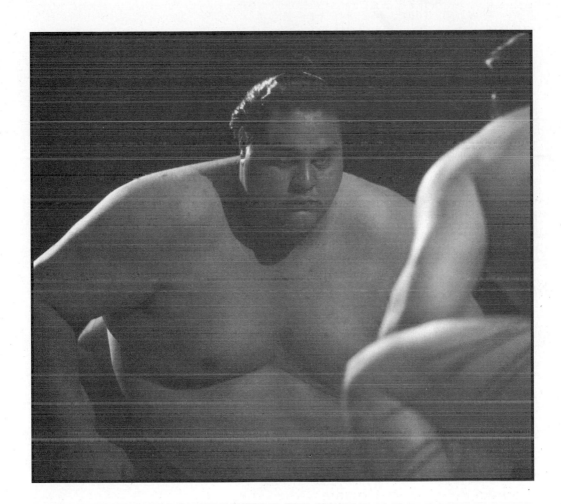

LESSON

Pre-reading Questions

1. Why do you think these men are so big?
2. Why are they looking at each other?
3. Do you ever watch this sport?

Sumo

Sumo wrestling is a national sport in Japan. Every year there are six **tournaments**, and millions of Japanese watch them on television. A tournament is a **series** of matches. | one after another

5 Sumo is almost as old as the nation of Japan itself. Stories say that there was sumo wrestling over two thousand (2,000) years ago. History says that there were national sumo tournaments in the eighth century.

10 Often, **athletes** are thin and can move very quickly. It is beautiful to watch them play. However, sumo wrestlers weigh from 100 to 160 kilos. One famous wrestler weighed 195 kilos. Sumo wrestlers do not look beautiful, 15 and sumo wrestling is a very slow sport. | people who play sports well

Sumo wrestlers start training when they are boys. They **exercise** to make their bodies strong. They also eat and eat and eat.

They wrestle in a round **ring** with a sand 20 floor. A wrestler loses the match if he leaves the ring. He is also the loser if any part of his body **except** his feet **touches** the floor. Each wrestler tries to push the other down on the floor or out of the ring. Sometimes one wrestler just **steps aside** 25 when the other wrestler **rushes** toward him. Then that wrestler falls down or falls out of the ring. | but

to the side
hurries

Sumo is not very popular in other countries, but the Japanese love it. Even young people find this traditional sport **exciting**. | exciting ≠ boring

A Vocabulary

Put the right word in the blanks. The sentences are from the text.

series	sumo wrestling	ring	except
steps	exercise	athletes	exciting
touches	aside	rushes	tournaments

1. Sometimes one wrestler just _____ _____ when the other wrestler _____ toward him.
2. A tournament is a _____ of matches.
3. He is also the loser if any part of his body _____ his feet _____ the floor.
4. _____ _____ is a national sport in Japan.
5. Even young people find this traditional sport _____.
6. Often _____ are thin and can move very quickly.
7. Every year there are six _____, and millions of Japanese watch them on television.
8. They wrestle in a round _____ with a sand floor.
9. They _____ to make their bodies strong.

B Vocabulary (new context)

Put the right word in the blanks.

athletes	wrestle	rushed	exciting
stepped	tournament	except	exercise
series	touch	aside	ring

1. Sumo is in a round _____. Thai boxing is in a square one.
2. Only two people box or _____ at the same time.
3. Stan put his math homework _____. He said he would do it later.
4. _____ play basketball, lacrosse, volleyball, and many other kinds of sports.
5. Everyone _____ Amahl is in class today. She is absent.
6. What number is missing from this _____? 3, 6, 12, 15
7. The students are organizing a ping pong _____. Sign up if you want to play.
8. Marie _____ from the Student Union to class because she was late.

9. In older elevators you have to push a button to make the elevator go. In new ones you just _____ the button.
10. Oscar told me some _____ news. He won a scholarship.
11. Walking and running are good _____.
12. John _____ on a piece of paper that was on the floor.

C Vocabulary Review

Match the words that are the opposite.

Column A
1. deliver _____
2. capture _____
3. straight _____
4. death _____
5. brave _____
6. loser _____
7. immediately _____
8. alive _____
9. kneel _____
10. national _____

Column B

a. later   g. dead
b. stand up   h. let go
c. international i. curved
d. winner   j. smooth
e. receive   k. afraid
f. goal   l. life

D Comprehension

Put a circle around the letter of the best answer.

1. Every year there are _____ sumo tournaments.
   a. 6   c. 160
   b. 15   d. 195

2. _____ says that there were sumo tournaments in the eighth century.
   a. A story   c. History
   b. An athlete   d. A wrestler

3. Most athletes are _____.
   a. heavy   c. thin
   b. overweight   d. smooth

4. Sumo wrestlers are _____.
   a. small   c. thin
   b. overweight   d. smooth

5. Sumo is a ———— sport.
   - a. fast
   - b. slow
   - c. comfortable
   - d. efficient

6. Sumo wrestlers ———— to make their bodies strong.
   - a. eat
   - b. swing
   - c. lose
   - d. exercise

7. Each wrestler tries to push the other ————.
   - a. down on the floor
   - b. out of the ring
   - c. into the air
   - d. a and b

8. The Japanese think that sumo is ————.
   - a. exciting
   - b. boring
   - c. embarrassing
   - d. pleasant

E Questions

The asterisk (*) means you have to think of the answer. You cannot find it in the text.

1. Where is sumo wrestling popular?
2. What is a tournament?
3. Is sumo an old sport?
4. How are sumo wrestlers different from other athletes?
5. How do sumo wrestlers train?
6. Describe a sumo ring.
7. How does a sumo wrestler lose the match?
*8. Is sumo exciting?
*9. Is it good for a person to weigh 160 or 195 kilos?

F Main Idea

Which is the main idea of this chapter? Choose one.

1. Sumo wrestling between two overweight men is a popular traditional sport in Japan.
2. The sumo wrestling ring is round and has a sand floor.
3. A sumo match is slow, and the wrestlers are very overweight.

Tarahumara Foot Races

LESSON

Pre-reading Questions

1. One woman is carrying a stick. The other is carrying a ring. Can you guess why?

2. Do you think the two women are on the same team. Why? Why not?

3. Do you like to run?

5

Tarahumara Foot Races

The Tarahumara live in the mountains in the state of Chihuahua in northern Mexico. This is an area of high mountains and deep tropical **valleys.** It sometimes snows in the
5   mountains in winter. The Tarahumara live in **caves,** or in wooden or stone houses. They have small farms. There are not many roads.

    Other Mexican tribes use horses or **donkeys** for travel. The Tarahumara walk **wherever** they
10   need to go. They carry heavy baskets on their **backs.** Perhaps this is why the Tarahumara are **excellent** runners. They can run many kilometers without getting tired, and they like to organize races.

15   When the men race, they kick a wooden ball **ahead** of them while they run. Before they start racing, they plan where and how long they will run. They might run just a few minutes, or they might run for several hours. Sometimes
20   they run in teams, and sometimes each person runs as an **individual.**

    The women's races are **similar** except that the women do not kick a ball. They throw a wooden **hoop** in front of them with a stick. A
25   hoop is a ring or **circle.**

    The Tarahumara have other games and sports. They even play a kind of lacrosse. However, they are famous because they can run so fast and so far.

low areas between mountains

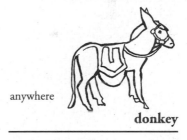

anywhere

donkey

very good

in front

one person

almost the same

A Vocabulary

Put the right word in the blanks. The sentences are from the text.

excellent	ahead	caves	wherever
hoop	circle	lacrosse	donkeys
backs	similar	valleys	individual

1. Other Mexican tribes use horses or _____ for travel.
2. When the men race, they kick a wooden ball _____ of them while they run.
3. This is an area of high mountains and deep tropical _____.
4. Perhaps this is why the Tarahumara are _____ runners.
5. They carry heavy baskets on their _____.
6. The women's races are _____ except that the women do not kick a ball.
7. They throw a wooden _____ in front of them with a stick.
8. A hoop is a ring or _____.
9. Sometimes they run in teams, and sometimes each person runs as an _____.
10. The Tarahumara walk _____ they need to go.
11. The Tarahumara live in _____, or in wooden or stone houses.

B Vocabulary (new context)

Put the right word in the blanks.

circle	valley	similar	donkeys
individually	backs	ahead	wherever
runners	excellent	caves	races

1. The teacher told the children to hold hands and form a large _____.
2. The sumo wrestler and the runner are both athletes, but they are not _____.
3. _____ can carry a lot on their _____, but sometimes they are lazy.
4. As Betty and Pat drove along the highway, they could see beautiful mountains _____ of them.
5. A _____ is a low area between two mountains.

6. Sometimes students answer questions in a group, and sometimes they answer _____.
7. Masako is an _____ student. She always gets good grades.
8. You will find English speakers _____ you go.

C Vocabulary Review

Put the right word in the blanks.

weapon	drum	proud	elbow
handle	swept	yell	fields
net	speeding	touch	athletes
excited	series	exercise	except

1. Helen _____ the floor after she washed the dishes.
2. Some people fish with a hook and line. Others use a _____.
3. Mr. and Mrs. Black have several _____ of corn on their farm.
4. You can open the desk drawer by pulling on the _____.
5. There are _____ from several countries in the competition for the world cup.
6. The children were _____ when they went to Disneyland.
7. It is important to eat good food and get lots of _____.
8. Tarahumara play a _____ while they dance.
9. Do all of the exercises _____ the last one. Don't do that one.
10. The first unit in this book has a _____ of lessons on animals.
11. The police stopped me because I was _____.

D Comprehension: True/False/No Information

Write T if the sentence is true. Write F if it is false. Write NI if no information is given.

_____ 1. Chihuahua is a state in Mexico.
_____ 2. It is hot in the valleys where the Tarahumara live.
_____ 3. They buy all their food in stores.
_____ 4. Some of the Tarahumara live in caves.

_____ 5. They cook their food outdoors.
_____ 6. The Tarahumara men are excellent runners, but the women are not.
_____ 7. The winners of the races receive money.
_____ 8. They usually race down the mountains.
_____ 9. The women kick a ball as they race.
_____ 10. The Tarahumara are famous because they play lacrosse.

E Questions

The asterisk (*) means you have to think of the answer. You cannot find it in the text.

1. Where do the Tarahumara live?
2. What is the land like there?
3. Does it ever snow?
4. Where do they get their food?
5. How do they travel?
6. How do most Mexican tribes travel?
7. Describe how the men race.
8. Do they always run in teams?
9. How is a women's race different from a men's race?
10. What is a hoop?
*11. Why are the Tarahumara excellent runners?

F Main Idea

Which is the main idea of this chapter? Choose one.

1. The Tarahumara live in caves and wooden and stone houses in the state of Chihuahua in Mexico.
2. The Tarahumara are excellent runners and can race for several hours without getting tired.
3. The Tarahumara women's races are similar to the men's.

Word Study

A Map Study

1. These are the seven continents: Africa, Antarctica, Asia, Australia, Europe, North America, and South America. Tell what continent these places are on. Use the map on page 223.

   a. Finland
   b. Egypt
   c. France
   d. Senegal
   e. Argentina

   f. Korea
   g. Burma
   h. Mount Everest
   i. Canada
   j. the South Pole

2. What countries are these places in? Use the map on page 223.

   a. Chihuahua
   b. Sarawak
   c. Rome
   d. Hokkaido
   e. New Mexico

   f. Arizona
   g. Chicago
   h. Ontario
   i. the Amazon River
   j. Alaska

B Compound Words

Make a compound word. Use a word from Column A and a word from Column B. Sometimes you can make two words.

Column A	Column B
1. birth	a. mate _____
2. table	b. how _____
3. day	c. bell _____
4. bed	d. cloth _____
5. grass	e. light _____
6. summer	f. land _____
7. some	g. day _____
8. door	h. time _____
9. team	i. room _____
10. sun	j. rise _____

C Word Forms

Verb	Noun	Adjective
1.	cube	cubic
2. move	movement	
3.	ability	able
4. free	freedom	free
5. dry	dryer	dry
6.	nation	national
	nationality	
7. excite	excitement	excited
8. think	thought	
9. run	running	
	runner	
10. please	pleasure	pleasant
		pleased

Put the correct word form in the blanks. Use a word from Line 1 in Sentence 1, and so on. Use the right verb forms and singular and plural nouns.

1. What is a _____? What does a _____ gram of water weigh?

2. A zipper _____ up and down. Each _____ opens or closes the hooks.

3. A chimney sweep has the _____ to breathe inside a chimney. He is _____ to do this because he wears air equipment.

4. The Burmese captured Naresuen. He won his _____ by boxing. Then he was _____. He returned to Thailand.

5. You can _____ your clothes in a clothes _____. When they are _____, take them out.

6. Where are you from? What is your _____? What does your _____ flag look like?

7. My cousin's family went to Disney World in Florida. The children were very _____. They got tired from all the _____.

8. What are you _____ about? Is your family in your _____ often?

9. Tom _____ five kilometers every morning. He is a fast
   _____. _____ is good for him.
10. This is a _____ city. I am _____ to be
    here.

D Past Tense Review

Write the past tense of these verbs.

1. step	6. speak	11. think
2. mix	7. try	12. grow
3. keep	8. meet	13. lose
4. lead	9. pay	14. shop
5. build	10. sell	15. send

E Irregular Verbs

Memorize these verbs. Then use the past tense of each verb in a sentence.

	Simple	Past		Simple	Past
1.	drive	drove	6.	slide	slid
2.	sweep	swept	7.	catch	caught
3.	drink	drank	8.	feel	felt
4.	fly	flew	9.	forget	forgot
5.	hear	heard	10.	run	ran

F Writing

Choose one or more of these topics and write answers.

1. Which sport in *Unit 2* is most interesting to you? Why?
2. Do you have a favorite sport? Do you play it or only watch it?
   Describe it.
3. In the United States, famous athletes in some popular sports, for
   example, football or baseball, earn a lot of money. In your country, do
   any famous athletes earn a lot of money? Who pays them? Do you
   think it is a good idea for famous athletes to earn a lot of money? Why
   or why not?

Video Highlights

A Before You Watch

1. You have read about Sumo wrestlers. Write down two facts that you already know about Sumo wrestlers.

©CNN

a. _____

b. _____

2. These words will help you understand the video. Read the words and their definitions.

    a. uniforms: special clothes worn by people belonging to a group
    b. lifestyle: the manner in which one lives
    c. career: a life's work, such as a teaching or business career
    d. opponent: a person on the opposite side in a game or contest
    e. Japan Sumo Association: the group to which many Sumo wrestlers belong

    Now choose one of the key words above for each of these sentences.

    a. Most Sumo wrestlers are members of the _____.
    b. Sumo wrestling is a two-thousand year old sport that doesn't fit into the _____ of many modern Japanese.
    c. Some young people don't like the strange _____ that all Sumo wrestlers must wear.
    d. A Sumo wrestler tries to push his _____ out of the ring.
    e. To train for their _____ of Sumo wrestling, young Japanese boys go to a school where they must study and exercise.

B As You Watch

1. What do you see in this video? Check the things that you see.

a. A child Sumo wrestler says "I don't like Sumo." _____

b. An older Japanese man talks about the uniforms the Sumo wrestlers wear. _____

c. A young girl gives her reasons for wanting to be a Sumo wrestler. _____

d. Young people dance in a night club. _____

e. A Sumo wrestler bows to the crowd. _____

f. A Sumo wrestler talks about his career. _____

g. A school run by the Japan Sumo Association. _____

h. Boys bow to their teacher, then sit down at their desks. _____

i. A Sumo wrestler eats his dinner. _____

j. A Sumo wrestling match. _____

k. Crowds cheer at the Sumo wrestling match. _____

C   After You Watch

1. **A Sumo wrestler, Mr. Ukita, is giving an interview to a journalist from the West.**

   Interviewer: When did you start your career of Sumo wrestling?

   Mr. Ukita: As a young boy. I went to a Sumo school.

   Interviewer: What did you learn at school besides wrestling?

   Mr. Ukita: Well, history, and—

   Interviewer: Eating?

   Mr. Ukita (laughs): Yes, eating as well. Unlike most people, Sumo wrestlers try to put on weight.

   Interviewer: I guess, from the look of the hairstyles and the strange uniforms you wear, that Sumo wrestling is a very traditional sport.

   Mr. Ukita: Yes, it goes way back. It's about two thousand years old.

   Interviewer: How do you decide which wrestler has won?

   Mr. Ukita: We have to push our opponents out of the ring. It's very difficult because they are all very heavy men.

Interviewer: Yes, I can see that. Now, I'd like to ask you a very personal question.

Mr. Ukita (laughs): I can guess what it is. Go ahead.

Interviewer: All right then. How much do you weigh?

Mr. Ukita: Well, the average wrestler weighs about 300 pounds. I weigh 148 kilos. That's just over 300 pounds. So I'm about the average for a Sumo wrestler.

Interviewer: That's a lot of Sumo wrestler there. Thanks for talking to me.

2. **Write five sentences with information contained in the interview above. Use reported speech.**

Example:
Mr. Ukita said that he learned history at school.

1. _____

2. _____

3. _____

4. _____

5. _____

Activity Page

A Sporting Needs

What do you need to play the six sports below?

SPORTS

tennis	basketball
ice hockey	curling
lacrosse	table tennis

Choose three items for each sport from the squares below and write a sentence.

Example: To play tennis you need a ball, a racket, and a court.

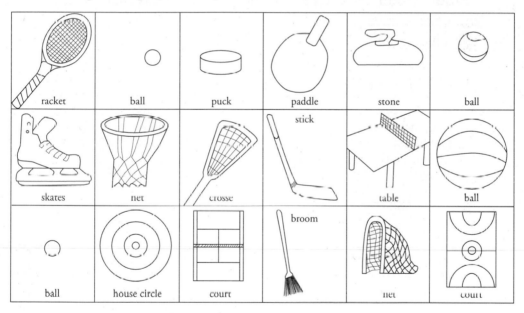

racket	ball	puck	paddle	stone	ball
skates	net	crosse	stick	table	ball
ball	house circle	court	broom	net	court

B What Sport Do I Play?

Read one of your activities to your partner without identifying the name of the sport. Your partner tries to guess the sport.

Example: To play this sport you need a court, a net, and a ball.

You can also do this activity with other sports.

Dictionary Page

Stress and Pronunciation

1. **Stress** If a word has more than one syllable, one of the syllables is stronger than the others. Your dictionary always has a ' in front of the stressed syllable. In the words below, say whether the stress is on the first, second, or third syllable. The first one is done for you.

'popular ___1___	'probably _____	ex'cept _____
'exercise _____	scien'tific _____	de'feated _____
'national _____	a'nother _____	'organize _____
a'side _____	un'usual _____	refu'gee _____

2. **Pronunciation** The strange writing you see on this page is phonetics. In our dictionary we call it the guide to pronunciation symbols. The phonetic spelling of the word is between the two slanted lines / / following each main entry. Look at the two entries below and write their normal spelling in the space provided.

_____ /'fridəm/ *noun*
1 having the power to act and speak without being stopped: *The boy has the freedom to go where he wants to go.*

_____ /raʊnd/ *adjective*
circular or curved in shape: *Balls are round.*

Now match the words in phonetics with the words in normal spelling. The first one is done for you.

Phonetic Spelling	Normal Spelling
1. /glʌvz/	a. round
2. /'saidwɔk/	b. match
3. /streit/	c. drum
4. /'ɛlboʊ/	d. sidewalk
5. /flæt/	e. straight
6. /'kæptən/	f. gloves
7. /drʌm/	g. freedom
8. /'fridəm/	h. elbow
9. /raʊnd/	i. captain
10. /mætʃ/	j. flat

Each sentence contains one word in phonetics. Its normal spelling is one of the three words that follow. Choose the correct word and underline it.

1. The lacrosse field is /ˈsɛvənti/ meters long. (seven, seventy, seventeen)
2. The players hit a ball /əˈraʊnd/ the field (around, along, another)
3. No part of his body except his feet touches the /flɔr/. (flat, floor, flute)
4. Young people find this traditional /spɔrt/ exciting. (sport, spirit, speed)
5. Sumo /ˈrɛslɪŋ/ is a Japanese sport. (rushing, rusting, wrestling)

Food

Context Clues

Put a circle around the letter of the best answer.

1. Betty hadn't done her French homework. That afternoon, she missed her French class **on purpose.**
   a. She wanted to miss class.
   b. She missed her class by accident.
   c. She thought her class was later.
   d. She got someone else to go to her class.

2. He made a **careless** mistake in his driving test and bumped into a tree. He must have been looking the other way.
   a. attentive
   b. thoughtless
   c. thoughtful
   d. normal

3. The cleaner **removed** all the dirt from the coat. It looked like new again.
   a. refused to take away
   b. repeated
   c. took away
   d. replaced

4. Your face is **familiar** to me, but I don't remember your name. You look like Margie White. Are you her sister?
   a. unknown
   b. closed
   c. known
   d. far away

5. The cross is a **sacred** symbol of the Christian religion. A lot of people bow their heads when they see it.
   a. forgotten
   b. happy
   c. everyday
   d. holy

6. Was your vacation a **pleasant** experience, or did the weather spoil it for you?
   a. agreeable
   b. hurtful
   c. harmful
   d. displeasing

7. One of the special **ingredients** in the spice cake is cinnamon. I think the others are nutmeg and cloves.
   a. mixtures
   b. list
   c. items
   d. values

8. Did Sean **discover** the person who broke open his locker? He was very upset when he told me about it.
   a. conceal
   b. bother about
   c. question
   d. find out

9. That wooden desk is **solid** oak. It will last for hundreds of years.
   a. It has a thin cover of oak.
   b. It is mostly oak.
   c. It's not real oak.
   d. It's all oak.

10. When Werner first arrived he wasn't used to the climate and caught cold after cold. But lately he seems to be in good heath. I guess he's **immune** by now.
    a. likely to catch
    b. unhealthy
    c. not affected
    d. in the hospital

11. I've **seldom** seen such bad behavior! They threw popcorn at each other, then talked all the way through the movie.
    a. rarely
    b. always
    c. often
    d. usually

12. He told her that job openings were **scarce,** and that they'd be lucky if they found work.
    a. frequent
    b. found easily
    c. limited
    d. unlimited

13. We ate most of the take-out Thai food for lunch and put the **remainder** in the refrigerator. Later we ate that for supper.
    a. rice
    b. essentials
    c. rest
    d. additions

14. I think she must be a **vegetarian.** I've never seen her eat meat.
    a. She eats only vegetables.
    b. She seldom eats vegetables.
    c. She only eats meat.
    d. She eats meat and vegetables.

15. If we're out of cream, use yogurt. It makes a good **substitute.**
    a. liquid
    b. replacement
    c. idea
    d. ingredient

The Puffer Fish

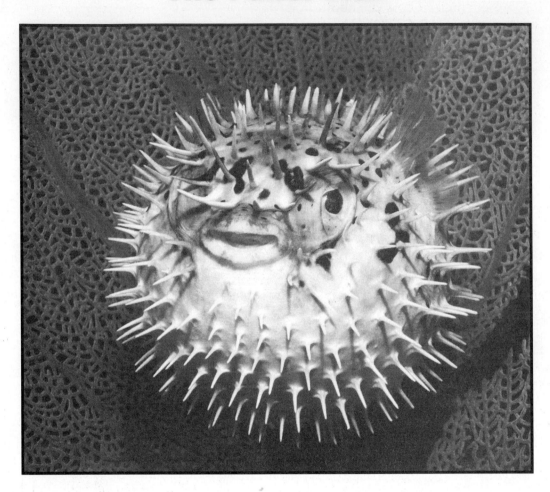

LESSON

1

Pre-reading Questions

1. Would you ever eat this fish? Why? Why not?

2. Why do you think it's called the puffer fish?

3. Do you have a favorite fish dish? What is it?

1

The Puffer Fish

Most people avoid eating dangerous foods. They don't want to get sick. However, there is one food that may be deadly, yet some people eat it **on purpose.** It's called the puffer fish.

5 This **species** of fish, called *fugu* in Japanese, lives in the Pacific Ocean. Some Japanese die every year from eating *fugu*. In fact, the Emperor of Japan is not allowed to touch it. Why? Well, the **insides** of the puffer fish are very poisonous.

10 They contain a venom 275 times more **powerful** than the deadly poison cyanide.

Usually nothing bad happens when *fugu* is on the menu. **Customers** leave the restaurant with happy smiles on their faces. The chefs are

15 trained to **remove** the insides of the puffer fish before they serve it to their customers. If they miss even a small **amount,** the fish is not safe to eat. If a chef is **careless,** the customers stop smiling and get sick.

20 Puffer fish is very expensive. A plate of *fugu* costs more than $200 in some restaurants in Tokyo. Besides this, the fish is very ugly, with spines all over its body. Also, it can puff itself up to double its **normal** size. That's the

25 **reason** for its name. Why do the Japanese **risk** so much for such an ugly and dangerous fish? Well, some people like taking risks. And *fugu* is **absolutely** delicious!

a group of living things

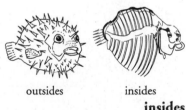

outsides   insides

insides

customers

average

A Vocabulary

Put the right word in the blanks. The sentences are from the text.

absolutely	on purpose	risk	reason
insides	powerful	remove	careless
normal	amount	customers	species

1. That's the _____ for its name.
2. Also, it can puff itself up to double its _____ size.
3. However, there is one food that may be deadly, yet some people eat it _____.
4. They contain a venom 275 times more _____ than the deadly poison cyanide.
5. If a chef is _____, the customers stop smiling and get sick.
6. _____ leave the restaurant with happy smiles on their faces.
7. Why do the Japanese _____ so much for such an ugly and dangerous fish?
8. Well, the _____ of the puffer fish are very poisonous.
9. This _____ of fish, called *fugu* in Japanese, lives in the Pacific Ocean.
10. The chefs are trained to _____ the insides of the puffer fish before they serve it to their customers.
11. And *fugu* is _____ delicious!
12. If they miss even a small _____, the fish is not safe to eat.

B Vocabulary (new context)

Put the right word in the blanks.

customers	remove	powerful	on purpose
amount	absolutely	insides	species
reason	careless	normal	risk

1. Heavy snow is _____ for Iceland at this time of year.
2. She took a _____ in having her purse stolen when she left it in that cafe.

3. Henry said he pushed me by accident, but I know he did it
   _____ .

4. I thought the singer was _____ fantastic.

5. The _____ they were late is that their bus had an accident.

6. He was so _____ with money that he was penniless within a year.

7. She may look shy and weak, but they say she's one of the most _____ people in banking.

8. Celia decided to _____ every trace of dust from the shelves before she started painting them.

9. With spiders, the female of the _____ is often more deadly than the male.

10. The _____ of money you save depends on how much you earn.

11. We ate so much pizza last night that our _____ were hurting.

12. So many _____ ate at Luigi's restaurant on the first evening that he decided to hire more waiters.

C Vocabulary Review

Put the right word in the blanks.

similar	arrived	individual	metric
gloves	captured	freedom	tournament
touch	exercise	trained	excellent

1. Helen _____ yesterday and her husband arrives today.

2. Can you do sit-ups? They're such good _____ .

3. Perez is innocent. After five years in prison he has the _____ to leave.

4. After a long search, the police _____ the criminal in the warehouse.

5. Can I borrow your _____ ? Mine are lost and my hands are freezing.

6. The dresses are _____ . They are the same color and style, but Nancy's has a matching belt.

7. There was a tennis _____ that day, but Philip had a cold and couldn't play.

8. Her written work was _____, but she failed the oral.
9. She _____ as a ballet dancer for five years before she appeared on stage.
10. "Don't you dare _____ that cake," the mother warned. "It's for our guests."
11. I want to learn the _____ system of measurement before I go to France next year.
12. One _____ walked away from the crowd of protesters.

D Comprehension: True/False/No Information

Write T if the sentence is true. Write F if it is false. Write NI if no information is given.

_____ 1. Puffer fish is eaten all around the world.
_____ 2. The Emperor of Japan eats *fugu* for his evening meal.
_____ 3. The most important task when preparing puffer fish is to remove its spines.
_____ 4. The puffer fish lives in the Pacific Ocean.
_____ 5. *Fugu* is popular because it is so cheap.
_____ 6. This fish can puff itself up to ten times its normal size.
_____ 7. There is some risk in eating a plate of *fugu*.
_____ 8. It is called the puffer fish in English because of the spines which cover its body.
_____ 9. The insides of the puffer fish are very poisonous.
_____ 10. All restaurants in Japan are expensive.

E Questions

The asterisk (*) means you have to think of the answer. You cannot find it in the text.

1. In what ocean does the puffer fish live?
*2. Is this ocean near Japan?
3. What parts of the puffer fish are poisonous?
4. Can the Emperor of Japan eat the puffer fish? Why? Why not?
5. Is cyanide poisonous? What is more deadly than cyanide?
6. In which country is *fugu* most popular?

7. What must chefs do before they serve the puffer fish?
8. How much does a plate of *fugu* cost in some restaurants?
*9. Why do you think *fugu* costs so much?
*10. Why do you think the puffer fish has spines over its body?

F Main Idea

Which is the main idea of this chapter? Choose one.

1. *Fugu* is one of the most expensive foods in the world.
2. Some people are willing to risk their lives to eat *fugu*.
3. Chefs must be carefully trained to prepare the puffer fish.

Foods from Around the World

A. ASIA (China)

B. EUROPE (Iceland)

C. AFRICA (Mali)

D. PACIFIC (Samoa)

LESSON

2

Pre-reading Questions

1. Which of the following would you use to eat the food in A, B, C, and D: chopsticks, fingers, knives and forks?

2. Which meal looks the most enjoyable? Why?

3. People spend a lot of time talking about food. Why do you think this is so?

Foods from Around the World

Foods that are well known to you may not be <u>familiar</u> to people from other countries. Here are four people's **experiences** with foreign food.

common, well-known

Shao Wong is a student in France. He
5 comes from China. "I'd never tasted cheese or even milk before I came here. Cattle are rare in my part of China, so there are no **dairy** products. I tried milk when I first arrived in France. I hated it! I sampled cheese too, but couldn't
10 **manage** more than one bite. I love ice cream, though, and that's made from milk."

dairy

Birgit is from Sweden. She traveled to Australia on vacation. "I was in a restaurant that specialized in fish, and I heard some other
15 customers **order** flake. So I ordered some too and it was delicious. Later, I found out that flake is an Australian **term** for shark. After that <u>pleasant</u> experience, whenever I see a new food I try it out on purpose. You know why? I
20 remember how much I enjoyed flake."

agreeable

Chandra is a dentist in Texas. She **originates** from India. "I'm frightened of eating new foods because they might be made from beef. I'm a Hindu, and my religion **forbids** me to
25 eat meat from the cow. It's a <u>sacred</u> animal to Hindus, so that's the reason I can't eat hamburgers or spaghetti with meatballs."

holy

Nathan is American. He taught for a year in China. "My friends gave me some 100-
30 year-old eggs to eat. I didn't like the look of them at all. The insides were green, but my friends said the color was normal. The Chinese put **chemicals** on fresh eggs. Then they **bury** them in the earth for three months.
35 So the eggs weren't really very old. Even so, I absolutely refused to touch them."

Life in a new country can be scary, but it also can be fun. Would you sample a 100-year-old egg? Would you order shark in a restaurant?

chemicals

A   Vocabulary

Put the right word in the blanks. The sentences are from the text.

bury	forbids	originates	pleasant
chemicals	sacred	familiar	experiences
dairy	term	order	manage

1. Then they _____ them in the earth for three months.
2. Later, I found out that flake is an Australian _____ for shark.
3. I'm a Hindu, and my religion _____ me to eat meat from the cow.
4. Foods that are well known to you may not be _____ to people from other countries.
5. The Chinese put _____ on fresh eggs.
6. After that _____ experience, whenever I see a new food I try it out on purpose.
7. It's a _____ animal to Hindus, so that's the reason I can't eat hamburgers or spaghetti with meatballs.
8. She _____ from India.
9. Here are four people's _____ with foreign food.

10. I sampled cheese too, but I couldn't _____ more than one bite.
11. I was in a restaurant that specialized in fish, and I heard some other customers _____ flake.
12. Cattle are rare in my part of China, so there are no _____ products.

B Vocabulary (new context)

Put the right word in the blanks.

experiences	dairy	pleasant	originates
chemicals	term	familiar	forbids
sacred	manage	order	bury

1. The school _____ its pupils to chew gum in the classroom.
2. Don't help me carry the box. I can _____ it alone.
3. Many people don't know that a lot of household cleaners contain dangerous _____.
4. The ceremony was so _____ that only members of the religion took part in it.
5. Her _____ in Alaska made her an expert on wildlife.
6. Ice cream is a _____ product, and so is cheese.
7. When our cat died, we decided to _____ him under the apple tree.
8. If we _____ a computer from that store, we'll get a month's supply of computer paper free.
9. We spent the afternoon with friends and then went out to eat in the evening. Altogether, it was a very _____ day.
10. We don't use the _____ "housewife" any more. Many women don't like it.
11. The Ganges River _____ in the Himalayas.
12. "His face looks _____ to me," said Arthur. "I've probably met him somewhere before."

C Vocabulary Review

Match the words that mean the same. The first is done for you.

Column A

1. series   _____g_____
2. careless   _____
3. remove   _____
4. exciting   _____
5. customer   _____
6. normal   _____
7. amount   _____
8. reason   _____
9. risk   _____
10. except   _____
11. tournament   _____
12. powerful   _____
13. exercise   _____

Column B

a. take away
b. total
c. purpose
d. competition
e. danger
f. mental or physical training
g. a group of similar things
h. expensive
i. independent
j. average
k. breathtaking, thrilling
l. thoughtless
m. buyer
n. strong
o. all but

D Comprehension: Multiple Choice

Put a circle around the letter of the best answer.

1. Some foods of other countries might be _____ to you.
   a. unfamiliar
   b. absolutely
   c. preserved
   d. willing

2. The Hindu religion forbids _____.
   a. green vegetables
   b. chemicals
   c. beef
   d. candy

3. Cattle are sacred to _____.
   a. Christians
   b. Jews
   c. Muslims
   d. Hindus

4. Hundred-year-old eggs are really only _____ old.
   a. three months
   b. thirty days
   c. three years
   d. three decades

5. In Australia, flake is another word for _____.
   a. octopus
   c. cheese
   b. hamburger
   d. shark

6. Ice cream is made from _____.
   a. cheese
   c. milk
   b. cattle
   d. fish

7. The insides of 100-year-old eggs are _____.
   a. green
   c. yellow
   b. white
   d. grey

E Questions

The asterisk (*) means you have to think of the answer. You cannot find it in the text.

1. Where does Shao Wong come from?
2. What foods did he sample when he first arrived in France?
3. Why did Birgit go to Australia?
*4. Do people from Sweden eat shark?
5. What made Birgit willing to try new foods?
6. Why was Chandra frightened of eating a hamburger?
7. Do Hindus eat beef? Why? Why not?
8. What was Nathan's country of origin?
9. Why wouldn't he sample 100-year-old eggs?
10. What do the Chinese put on eggs to preserve them?
11. What was the real age of the eggs?
*12. Do the Chinese generally eat butter?

F Main Ideas

Which is the main idea of this chapter? Choose one.

1. A vacation is a good way to learn about new foods.
2. Foods that might be familiar to you are unknown to people from other countries.
3. Many people dislike eating new foods because their religion forbids it.

Chocolate

A.

B.

LESSON

Pre-reading Questions

1. Photos A and B are connected in some way. How?

2. Can you name some foods that use chocolate?

3. Many people say chocolate is their favorite food. Why do you think this is?

3

Chocolate

We now think of chocolate as sweet, but once it was **bitter**. We think of it as a candy, but once it was a **medicine.** Today, chocolate can be a hot drink, a frozen dessert, or just a
5 **snack.** Sometimes it's an **ingredient** in the main course of a meal. Mexicans make a hot chocolate sauce called mole and pour it over chicken. The Mexicans also eat chocolate with spices like chili peppers.

10 Chocolate is a **product** of the tropical cacao tree. The beans taste so bitter that even the monkeys say "ugh!" and run away. Workers must first dry and then roast the beans. This removes the bitter taste.

15 The word "chocolate" comes from a Mayan word. The Mayas were an **ancient** people who once lived in Mexico. They **valued** the cacao tree. Some used the beans for money, while others **crushed** them to make a drink.

20 When the Spaniards came to Mexico in the sixteenth century, they started drinking cacao too. Because the drink was strong and bitter, they thought it was a medicine. No one had the idea of adding sugar. The Spaniards
25 took some beans back to Europe and opened cafes. Wealthy people drank cacao and said it was good for the **digestion.**

bitter ≠ sweet

ingredient

very old

cacao beans

crushed

In the 1800s the owner of a chocolate factory in England **discovered** that sugar removed
30 the bitter taste of cacao. It quickly became a cheap and popular drink. Soon afterward, a factory made the first <u>**solid**</u> block of sweetened chocolate. Later on, another factory mixed milk and chocolate together. People liked the taste of
35 milk chocolate even better.

solid ≠ liquid, gas

Besides the chocolate candy bar, one of the most popular American snacks is the chocolate-chip cookie. **Favorite** desserts are chocolate cream pie and, of course, an ice cream sundae
40 with hot fudge sauce.

A Vocabulary

Put the right word in the blanks. The sentences are from the text.

solid	snack	discovered	bitter
digestion	favorite	product	valued
ancient	medicine	ingredient	crushed

1. In the 1800s the owner of a chocolate factory in England
    _____ that sugar removed the bitter taste of cacao.
2. Wealthy people drank cacao and said it was good for the
    _____.
3. They _____ the cacao tree.
4. Soon afterward, a factory made the first _____ block of
    sweetened chocolate.
5. _____ desserts are chocolate cream pie and, of course, an
    ice cream sundae with hot fudge sauce.
6. We now think of chocolate as sweet, but once it was
    _____.
7. We think of it as a candy, but once it was a _____.

8. Today, chocolate can be a hot drink, a frozen dessert, or just a _____.

9. Some used the beans for money, while others _____ them to make a drink.

10. Chocolate is a _____ of the tropical cacao tree.

11. Sometimes it's an _____ in the main course of a meal.

12. The Mayas were an _____ people who once lived in Mexico.

B Vocabulary (new context)

Put the right word in the blanks.

medicine	product	ancient	solid
digestion	favorite	valued	snack
crushed	discovered	ingredient	bitter

1. Mrs. Mendez said Pavarotti was her _____ singer. Her daughter chose Madonna.

2. The main _____ of IBM is computers.

3. The lemonade was so _____ that nobody wanted to drink it.

4. The Smithsons _____ some dinosaur bones on their farm.

5. A glass of milk after meals is supposed to help the _____.

6. The doctor knew that the boy didn't like _____, so he added sugar.

7. Most _____ civilizations had some sort of writing system.

8. The huge machines _____ the stones to make gravel for the new road.

9. The family _____ the chair very highly, because it belonged to their grandfather.

10. I'm so hungry! And I didn't even bring a _____ with me!

11. The main _____ in that cake is chocolate.

12. The pond is frozen _____. We can go skating.

C Vocabulary Review

Put the right word in the blanks.

sacred	valleys	order	ahead
teammates	manage	forbids	pleasant
originates	experiences	dairy	chemicals

1. Cows are milked at the _____ each morning.
2. The _____ he had in building tree houses as a child led him to architecture in later life.
3. The _____ are still covered in snow at this time of year.
4. They can _____ the easy lessons by themselves, but they'll need help with the harder ones.
5. She kept her father's photo. His memory was _____ to her.
6. This delicious goat cheese _____ from Greece.
7. A town law _____ us to park on that side of the street.
8. The _____ in some food products can be harmful to our health.
9. The trip was a _____ experience for all the family except Grandma. She found the weather too hot.
10. "Why do you think you can _____ me around like that?" asked Jason. "You're not my father."
11. In basketball you have four _____ to help you, in curling you have three.
12. What's that in the road _____? Not another traffic jam!

D Comprehension: True/False/No Information

Write T if the sentence is true. Write F if it is false. Write NI if no information is given.

_____ 1. The Spaniards arrived in Mexico in the seventeenth century.
_____ 2. Chocolate was always considered a sweet food.
_____ 3. It wasn't until the twentieth century that sugar was added to chocolate.
_____ 4. The cacao tree grows in tropical countries.
_____ 5. Because chocolate was bitter, people thought it was a medicine.
_____ 6. The Mayas lived in Argentina.

_____ 7. The Mayas used the cacao beans as ornaments.
_____ 8. Workers must soak the cacao beans before they can be used.
_____ 9. In the Philippines, people drink chocolate for breakfast.
_____ 10. People once believed chocolate was good for the digestion.
_____ 11. When milk and sugar were added to chocolate, people liked the taste even better.

E Questions

The asterisk (*) means you have to think of the answer. You cannot find it in the text.

√ 1. Was chocolate once a medicine? What did it taste like? *bitter*
√*2. Does the cacao tree grow in Canada? Why? Why not? *No, it doesn't. Cacao tree grow in warm place.*
√ 3. Can you eat the cacao beans? Why? Why not? *No, I can't. Cacao beans taste so bitter.*
√ 4. What do workers do to the beans? Why? *They must first dry and then roast the beans.*
√ 5. Where does the word "chocolate" come from? *Mayan*
  6. Who were the Mayas?
  7. Where did they live?
  8. What uses did they find for the beans?
  9. When did the Spaniards come to Mexico?
 10. How did the cacao bean arrive in Europe?
 11. What was added to chocolate to make it more popular?
 12. What are some popular foods that use chocolate as an ingredient?

F Main Idea

Which is the main idea of this chapter? Choose one.

1. Over the years, chocolate has developed from a bitter medicine to a popular snack.
2. The Spaniards brought the cacao bean from Mexico to Europe.
3. Although chocolate originates in the tropics, it is now sold in cool climates.

The Healthy Hunza

LESSON

4

Pre-reading Questions

1. Does this man look healthy? Why? Why not?

2. Is a city or a village the healthier place to live in? Why?

3. Who is the oldest person you know? How old is she or he? Is the person in good health?

The Healthy Hunza

For a long time, people believed there was a place in the Himalayas where the **inhabitants** lived forever. They called the place Shangri-La. This name came to mean **"paradise"** in the
5 English language.

    A lot of the stories about Shangri-La are **untrue.** However, some are **accurate.** The original Shangri-La was the Hunza Valley, a **remote** region in the high mountains of northern
10 Pakistan. The Hunza people don't live forever, but many live to be over one hundred years old. They appear to be among the healthiest people in the world. They are certainly **immune** to the many diseases of this area.

15   Why is this? People who have traveled to this remote area say it's because the Hunza **diet** is so healthy. The inhabitants eat only what they grow. Grain, fruit and vegetables are their daily food. They **seldom** eat butter or eggs. They eat
20 meat only on important feast days. Their only sweet dish is dried apricots. The Hunza never drink **alcohol.** Their religion forbids it. Sugar and canned food are also unknown to them.

    There are two other reasons why the
25 Hunza diet is so healthy. Firstly, there are few trees in the high mountains of the Hunza

people who live in an area

far away

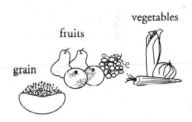

diet of the Hunza

region, so wood for the kitchen stove is **scarce.**   rare
This means that the inhabitants must cook
their food quickly. Doctors now say that short
30 cooking times are best for a healthy diet.
Secondly, the Hunza have a **limited** area of
farmland. Their valley is only one mile wide
because it lies between some very high mountains. They can never grow extra crops, and as a
35 result their food is carefully **rationed.** That is
why you never see an overweight Hunza.

A Vocabulary

Put the right word in the blanks. The sentences are from the text.

inhabitants	paradise	immune	diet
untrue	alcohol	limited	scarce
accurate	remote	seldom	rationed

1. The original Shangri-La was the Hunza Valley, a _____
   region in the high mountains of northern Pakistan.
2. Secondly, the Hunza have a _____ area of farmland.
3. This name came to mean _____ in the English language.
4. The Hunza never drink _____.
5. People who have traveled to this remote area say it's because the Hunza
   _____ is so healthy.
6. They can never grow extra crops, and as a result their food is carefully

   _____.

7. A lot of the stories about Shangri-La are _____.
8. They are certainly _____ to the many diseases of this
   area.
9. They _____ eat butter or eggs.
10. Firstly, there are few trees in the high mountains of the Hunza region, so
    wood for the kitchen stove is _____.
11. However, some are _____.
12. For a long time people believed there was a place in the Himalayas
    where the _____ lived forever.

B Vocabulary (new context)

Put the right word in the blanks.

accurate   paradise   seldom   untrue
diet   remote   immune   rationed
scarce   alcohol   limited   inhabitants

1. In wartime, people had to produce cards to get meat, butter and other _____ goods.
2. Once you've had measles, you're _____ for the rest of your life.
3. Their free time was _____ to an hour every day.
4. The nomads of the Sahara live in _____ desert regions.
5. A few religions forbid the drinking of _____.
6. "Still on your _____?" asked Brenda. "You don't seem to have lost any weight."
7. The tourist brochures called the tropical island a _____.
8. Most of what he says is _____. Very few people believe him.
9. Sam _____ goes to the theater, but he often goes to the cinema.
10. There were now only fifty male _____ left. The others had gone to work in the nearest big city.
11. I doubt that those numbers are _____. I'm sure there are more than three thousand voters living here.
12. Food is _____ in times of famine.

C Vocabulary Review

Match the words that are the opposite. The first is done for you.

Column A

1. solid   ____k____
2. insides   _____
3. normal   _____
4. on purpose _____
5. powerful   _____

Column B

a. sweet
b. crowded
c. whispers
d. weak
e. wouldn't

Column A		Column B
6. gave	_____	f. received
7. would	_____	g. soon
8. bitter	_____	h. departed
9. deserted	_____	i. strange
10. forbids	_____	j. queen
11. yells	_____	k. liquid
12. arrived	_____	l. outsides
13. king	_____	m. allows
		n. royalty
		o. by accident

D Comprehension: Multiple Choice

Put a circle around the letter of the best answer.

1. Shangri-La came to mean _____ in the English language.
   a. Himalayas
   b. Pakistan
   c. paradise
   d. Hunza

2. The Hunza people live in a remote _____ in northern Pakistan.
   a. valley
   b. coastal area
   c. desert
   d. steppe

3. The Hunza are _____ to the many diseases of this area.
   a. forbidden
   b. rationed
   c. limited
   d. immune

4. The Hunza eat only what they can _____ themselves.
   a. buy
   b. import
   c. grow
   d. observe

5. They _____ eat butter and eggs.
   a. seldom
   b. continually
   c. often
   d. always

6. Wood for cooking food is _____.
   a. scarce
   b. forbidden
   c. plentiful
   d. unknown

7. There is a _____ area of farming land in the Hunza valley.
   a. large
   b. limited
   c. plentiful
   d. unknown

8. The people have to _____ their food.
   a. keep
   b. guard
   c. ration
   d. give away

9. It's difficult to find a Hunza who is _____
   a. not overweight
   b. overweight
   c. accurate
   d. healthy

E Questions

The asterisk (*) means you have to think of the answer. You cannot find it in the text.

1. What does Shangri-La mean in English?
2. Is the story of Shangri-La true?
3. Where is the Hunza valley?
4. Do the Hunza catch diseases easily?
5. What do travelers say about the Hunza diet?
6. Can you name some of the daily foods of the Hunza?
7. Why is alcohol forbidden to them?
8. Are there many canned foods in the Hunza Valley? *Why do you think this is?
9. There are two reasons why the Hunza diet is so healthy. What is one?
10. Why must the inhabitants cook their food quickly?
11. What do doctors now say about short cooking times?
*12. Can you name some other rules for a healthy diet?

F Main Idea

Which is the main idea of this chapter? Choose one.

1. The Hunza people are religious and that keeps them in good health.
2. The long life of the Hunza is due in part to their healthy diet.
3. Now people know that the story of Shangri-La is not all legend.

Food of the Future?

LESSON

5

Pre-reading Questions

1. Where do you think this man is?

2. Why is the food on a tray?

3. Can you think of any other places where food is served on a tray?

Food of the Future?

Scientists are always trying out new ways of growing food, but even they can only guess what food will be like in the future. You can perhaps get a better **focus** on what lies ahead
5 from the four ideas below. Read them and see if you can guess what the future hamburger will taste like.

The sea can be farmed. Only one third of the earth's area is land. The **remainder** is
10 sea. The ocean contains huge amounts of tiny sea-animals called krill. Krill are already in some fish products, such as fish sticks and canned crab. Next time you buy canned or frozen seafood look carefully at the **label.**
15 You might see krill listed as one of the ingredients. Seaweed is another **source** of future food from the ocean. It is used in ice cream and some breads.

Animals can be changed. A farmer is able
20 to "engineer" his animals by adding **hormones** to their feed. Hormones can make chicken meat more tender or beef less fat. For example, dairy farmers add growth hormones so that calves produce milk sooner than normal.

25 New crops can be planted. Today, rice **supports** more than half the world's population.

what is left over

*growth **hormones** make calves grow more quickly*

hormones

*soybeans can be used as a **substitute** for meat*

source

supports

But it takes a lot of water to grow rice. Scientists **predict** the climate will get drier during the next century. Therefore, it might be impossible

30 to grow rice in the future. Some farmers are **experimenting** with new crops. Farmers like to grow beans because they don't need much water, and beans also **improve** the quality of the soil. The soybean makes a good <u>substitute</u> for rice

35 and meat. People can now eat soyburgers in some restaurants.

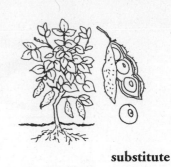

substitute

Plants can be grown inside. Some vegetables are now grown without soil and under <u>artificial</u> light. In Japan, there is an indoor lettuce farm

made by humans

40 run by machines and computers. The lettuce travels along slowly moving belts toward a super-market next door. By the time the lettuce is ready, it's outside the supermarket door. Five minutes later, shoppers can buy fresh lettuce.

45 So what is the future hamburger to be like? Let's go there and see. The bun is light and toasty, even though it began life as seaweed. On the bun there is some fresh green lettuce that grew under artificial light. The patty is made

50 from soybean, not from beef. Everyone is **vegetarian** because it's healthier. On top of the soybean patty is a slice of cheese made from the milk of engineered cows. The ketchup is also different. The writing on the label says,

55 "*Krillup.* Made from highest quality krill."

A Vocabulary

Put the right word in the blanks. The sentences are from the text.

artificial   vegetarian   substitute   label
experimenting   remainder   source   focus
improve   predict   supports   hormones

1. Next time you buy canned or frozen seafood, look carefully at the
   _____.
2. Some farmers are _____ with new crops.
3. Farmers like to grow beans because they don't need much water, and
   beans also _____ the quality of the soil.
4. Some vegetables are now grown without soil and under
   _____ light.
5. A farmer is able to "engineer" his animals by adding
   _____ to their feed.
6. The _____ is sea.
7. Everyone is _____ because it's healthier.
8. Today, rice _____ more than half the world's population.
9. Scientists _____ the climate will get drier during the
   next century.
10. The soybean makes a good _____ for rice and meat.
11. You can perhaps get a better _____ on what lies ahead
    from the four ideas below.
12. Seaweed is another _____ of future food from the ocean.

B Vocabulary (new context)

Put the right word in the blanks.

improve   vegetarian   source   label
hormones   supports   focus   substitute
remainder   predict   artificial   experimenting

1. The leading actor had a cold and couldn't speak. A _____
   actor took his place.
2. Journalists often refuse to disclose the _____ for their
   reports.

3. During the performance, _____ snow was used. Under the theater lights it looked almost real.

4. My teenage son is out of control. I blame it on his _____.

5. Mrs. Bartelmy _____ her entire family by working twelve hours a day.

6. The _____ on the jar was so old we could barely read the writing.

7. "I _____ a very happy future for you," said the fortune teller.

8. Read your text for the _____ of the hour.

9. Many scientists are _____ with food products to see if they are able to discover something new.

10. We were able to _____ better on our work when there was no noise outside.

11. Of course she couldn't eat the steak! She's a _____.

12. I hope we can _____ our performance tonight. A lot of the players were nervous last night.

■C■ Vocabulary Review

Put the right word in the blanks.

scarce	familiar	seldom	amount
ring	accurate	remote	ancient
inhabitants	paradise	rationed	immune

1. In the package was a very expensive gold _____. She immediately put it on her finger.

2. Most of the _____ of Brazil speak Portuguese.

3. The tropical flowers and the beautiful people make the island of Tahiti a _____.

4. Her name was _____ to Robert. He thought they might belong to the same club.

5. The _____ of food you eat determines how much you weigh.

6. Water is very _____ in dry countries.

7. "I _____ see my children any more," he grumbled. "Just once a year on my birthday."

8. That hotel is so _____ only a few travelers ever stay there.
9. The _____ bones of the dinosaur crumbled and broke.
10. *The Daily Times* is usually _____ in its reporting. It's *The Post* you can't trust.
11. During the past month, they _____ themselves to only one piece of candy a day.
12. I'm told if you take lots of vitamin C you'll be _____ from colds all winter.

D Comprehension: True/False/No Information

Write T if the sentence is true. Write F if it is false. Write NI if no information is given.

1. Two thirds of the earth's area is sea.
2. There is very little krill left in the ocean.
3. Seaweed is another source of our future food.
4. Growth hormones stop cows from giving milk.
5. Beans destroy the quality of the soil.
6. Rice supports more than half the earth's population.
7. Scientists predict that the earth will get windier in the next hundred years.
8. Rice needs more water than most other grain crops.
9. Soybeans are already being used as a substitute for meat and rice.
10. All plants need soil and sunlight to make them grow.
11. Vegetarians usually eat meat in the evening.

E Questions

The asterisk (*) means you have to think of the answer. You cannot find it in the text.

*1. How much of the earth's surface is land?
2. What are two products that come from krill?
3. What are two foods we can farm from the ocean?
4. Is it possible for scientists to change animals? How?
5. What do some farmers do to improve milk production?
6. Is rice important as a crop? Why?
7. What do scientists predict for the next century?

8. Why do some farmers choose beans as a crop?
9. What product is a substitute for rice and meat? Can you already eat food made from this product?
10. Are soil and natural light always necessary to grow plants?
11. Can you name an ingredient in the hamburger of the future?
*12. Can you name some foods that vegetarians eat?

F Main Ideas

Which is the main idea of this chapter? Choose one.

1. Millions of people are hungry because they don't have enough to eat.
2. We are searching for new ways to increase food production.
3. More restaurants are serving artificial food.

Word Study

A Count/Noncount Nouns

We classify nouns as count nouns or noncount nouns. Count nouns have a singular form and a plural form. Noncount nouns have a singular form only. They do not have a plural form.

Examples:

Count Nouns
I had an unusual **experience** yesterday.
Her **experiences** in China were interesting.
A **customer** just came in the store.
There are three **customers** in the store.

Noncount Nouns
Don't forget to take your **medicine.**
Medicine is expensive.
The **food** here is delicious.
There is a lot of **food** on the table.

Use a word from the chart to complete each sentence below.

Count nouns		Noncount nouns
ingredient	ingredients	alcohol
chemical	chemicals	remainder
customer	customers	medicine
reason	reasons	cost
		money

1. Are there any _____ missing from this recipe?
2. Where is the _____ of our meal?
3. Is there _____ in Bertha's drink?
4. What are the most dangerous _____ in the world?
5. Is this _____ from your doctor?
6. Is the _____ of food going up?
7. Do you have a _____ for refusing to eat?
8. Is there any _____ in my wallet?

B Adjectives with *-able*

Add the suffix *-able* to these verbs to form adjectives. Write the adjectives in the blanks.

Verb	Adjective
detest	_____
manage	_____
predict	_____
reason	_____

Drop the final *-e* on these verbs and then add the suffix *-able*. Write the adjectives in the blanks.

Verb	Adjective
remove	_____
value	_____
measure	_____
believe	_____

Can you think of an example of each of these?

The first one is done for you.

1. Something valuable.   *Gold is valuable.*
2. Something unbelievable.   _____
3. Something measurable.   _____
4. Something usable in the kitchen.   _____
5. Something enjoyable.   _____

C Word Forms

	Verb	Noun	Adjective
1.	remain	remainder	
2.	risk	risk	risky
3.	originate	origin	
4.	inhabit	inhabitant	
5.	digest	digestion	
6.	ration	rations	
7.	produce	product	

Verb	Noun	Adjective
8. value	value	valuable
9.	medicine	medicinal

Put the correct word form in the blanks. Use a word from Line 1 in Sentence 1, and so on. Use the right verb forms and singular and plural nouns.

1. If you subtract ninety from one hundred, the _____ is ten. If you have fifty dollars and you spend twenty, how much money _____?

2. It's too _____ to climb that rock in the rain. It's all right to take a _____ sometimes, but that would be madness. I just can't _____ it.

3. Do you know the _____ of ice cream? Some people say that ice cream _____ in China.

4. Legend says that the _____ of Shangri-La live forever. They _____ a remote region of Pakistan.

5. Is that meat easy to _____? If it isn't, I will have to take something to help my _____.

6. The Hunza people have to be careful with their _____. They _____ their food to last them through the winter.

7. Chocolate is a _____ of the cacao tree. It grows large pods on its trunk, and the pods _____ dozens of beans.

8. I'm sure your necklace is very _____. What _____ did the jeweler place on it? I'm sure you _____ it very highly.

9. The doctor prescribed a _____ drink. It tasted more like a soft drink than _____.

D Past Tense Review

Write the past tense of these verbs.

1. bury
2. improve
3. originate
4. value
5. discover
6. label
7. predict
8. experiment
9. substitute
10. support
11. ration
12. digest
13. crush
14. manage
15. focus

E Writing

Choose one or more of these topics and write answers.

1. What's your favorite food? Why do you like it?
2. What is a popular holiday food in your country? Why is it so popular?
3. Not everyone in the world has a healthy diet. What are some of the reasons for this?

Video Highlights

A Before You Watch

1. You've read about the puffer fish.
   Now read the five sentences below.
   Write *T* if the sentence is true.
   Write *F* if it is not true.

   _____ a. The puffer fish is one of
   the most poisonous
   creatures in the world.
   _____ b. The puffer fish can double itself in size.
   _____ c. The puffer fish is found off the coast of Canada.
   _____ d. The puffer fish is a favorite food of Central America.
   _____ e. The puffer fish is called *fugu* in Japanese.

2. These words will help you understand the video. Read the words
   and their definitions.

   a. cyanide: a deadly poison
   b. gourmet: an expert on fine food
   c. licensed: permitted by the government or an official group
   d. antidote: a cure for poison
   e. auctioneer: a person in charge of public sales

Choose one of the words above for each of the sentences.

   a. She refused to eat at fast-food restaurants because she was a
   _____.
   b. The _____ sold the house for $500,000.
   c. That restaurant is _____ to sell alcohol.
   d. The poison of the puffer fish is hundreds of times more deadly
   than _____.
   e. There is an _____ for most poisonous snake bites,
   but none for the puffer fish poison.

B As You Watch

You will see five places in the video. In each place, different people are doing different activities. As you watch, draw a line and connect the place with the people and the activities. One is done for you.

Place	People	Activity
fish market	chefs	put live puffer fish in trays
restaurant	cutters	arrange *fugu* on a plate
fish factory	buyers and sellers	eat *fugu*
auction	workers	put their hands under a cloth
restaurant kitchen	diners	remove insides of puffer fish

C After You Watch

1. The people who sell puffer fish say that no more than a dozen people die each year from eating it. But some journalists and other writers say that more than one hundred people die every year.

   a. The video interviewer said that only about a dozen people die of eating *fugu* every year. Whose side did he take? Write a sentence to show your view.

   _____

2. In the video, a puffer fish seller said he wanted to export *fugu* to other countries. He said that all the poisonous insides are removed from the puffer fish and it is no longer dangerous.

   a. Work with a partner. Partner A is a puffer fish seller and Partner B is a journalist. Choose your partner and write the rest of the discussion.

Partner A (puffer fish seller):
Puffer fish is delicious. I want to sell it to Canada, Mexico, the United States—

Partner B (journalist):
Wait a moment. I have a book that says over 100 people die every year from eating puffer fish—

_____   _____
_____   _____
_____   _____

_____   _____
_____   _____
_____   _____
_____   _____
_____   _____
_____   _____

b. Does the puffer fish seller have the right to export his fish? Is the journalist right to say the puffer fish is dangerous? Take a vote with the rest of the class and see who wins.

Activity Page

Draw the Word

A. Nathan, Birgit, Shao Wong, and Chandra are ordering food in a restaurant. Read what they're saying about their likes and dislikes, then choose a meal for each person.

Shao Wong **Chandra** **Nathan** **Birgit**

I hate dairy products.

I can't eat meat or fish.

I like most foods except eggs.

I love unusual foods.

Menu

Appetizers
Mixed Salad
100-Year-Old Eggs
Creamed Beef on Toast
Cheese Puffs

Main Course
Roast Beef with Vegetables
Fish with Cream Sauce
Soyburger with Salad
Lobster Mayonnaise

Soup
Shark Fin
Cheese and Onion
Beef and Noodle
Egg and Sweet Corn

Dessert
Chocolate Cream Pie
Fresh Apricots
Cheese and Crackers
Ice-cream Sundae

Shao Wong	Chandra	Nathan	Birgit
Appetizer	*Appetizer*	*Appetizer*	*Appetizer*
Soup	*Soup*	*Soup*	*Soup*
Main Course	*Main Course*	*Main Course*	*Main Course*
Dessert	*Dessert*	*Dessert*	*Dessert*

B. Pretend you're one of the four people above. Order a meal. Your partner has to guess which of the four people you are.

Example: For an appetizer I'd like 100-Year-Old Eggs. Then I think I'll have Shark-Fin soup. For my main course I'm going to choose . . . (Birgit)

Dictionary Page

Parts of speech

1. The dictionary entries below contain different parts of speech (noun, verb, adverb or adjective). One is circled. Circle the other four.

   accuracy /'ækyərəsi/ *noun*
   1 something that is correct and true: *the accuracy of a report*
   2 the ability to hit a target: *Her accuracy with the gun surprised everyone.*
   accurate /'ækyərɪt/ *adjective*
   exact, correct: *the numbers in the report are accurate.* —*adverb* **accurately**.

   experience /ɪk'spɪriəns/ *noun*
   1 an event: *Our visit to Alaska was a pleasant experience.*
   2 understanding gained through doing something: *She has years of experience in teaching.*
   experience *verb* **experienced, experiencing, experiences** to feel or know by personal involvement in: *She has experienced difficulties (satisfaction, success, etc.) in her new job.*

2. Choose a word from the entries above and put it in the sentences below. Use the correct verb form, and singular or plural nouns.

   a. He wrote about his many strange ———————— of living in the desert.

   b. I hope Jeffrey takes the time to write his report ————————.

   c. The remarks he made about the book are funny but ————————.

   d. She hit the ball with such ———————— that she almost always won at tennis.

   e. They ———————— severe stomach pain after eating the leftover food.

3. In the dictionary entries below, the parts of speech are missing. Read each entry carefully and then write whether the word is a noun, verb, adjective, or adverb in the space provided.

origin /ˈɔrədʒɪn/ ( )
the start or beginning of something true: *The origin of that folk song is France.*

original /əˈrɪdʒənəl/ ( )
1 first, earliest: *The original draft of her novel has been lost.*
2 new, different from what has come before: *That book has many original ideas.*
3 not a copy or translation: *The original painting is in a museum; this is just a copy.*

original ( )
something that cannot be or has not been copied or translated: *She wants to study English, so she can read Shakespeare's plays in the original.*

originally /əˈrɪdʒənəli/ ( )
previously, before: *He originally came from Florida but lives in Chicago now.*

valuable /ˈvælyuəbəl/ ( )
1 having worth, value: *Gold jewlery is valuable.*
2 useful, helpful: *a valuable piece of information*

valuables ( )
personal objects, such as jewelry or art: *She keeps her valuables in a safe.*

value /ˈvælyu/ ( )
valued, valuing, values
1 to think something is important: *I value my best friend's advice.*
2 to put a price on something: *An expert valued the painting at $1 million.*

value ( )
1 worth: *The value of this home has doubled since we have owned it.*
2 *plural* ideals, standards of a society: *We have tried to teach our children values like honesty and hard work.*

Mysteries

Context Clues

Choose the lettered answer that means the same as the word in bold.

1. At midnight there was a loud knock on the door. When Ali opened it no one was there. It was a **mystery.**
   a. Ali couldn't explain the knock.
   b. Ali knew the answer.
   c. Ali was annoyed that his neighbor knocked on the door so late.
   d. Ali laughed at the joke.

2. The sailors rowed over to the strange ship. No one came to meet them. The ship seemed **deserted.**
   a. The people on the ship were eating their dessert.
   b. The ship was damaged.
   c. No one was on the ship.
   d. The ship had produce from hot desert lands.

3. Yuri opened his **diary** and turned to a new page. What had happened that day? He thought for a few minutes and then began to write.
   a. a record of the day's events   c. a daily newspaper
   b. daily physical exercise   d. a shopping list

4. No one was able to **solve** the puzzle. It remains a mystery.
   a. repeat   c. take away
   b. explain   d. replace

5. Sara makes up stories and poems about the future. She has a wonderful **imagination.**
   a. knowledge   c. mental ability
   b. creative ability   d. mathematical ability

6. When the computer crashed for the third time, Wei stopped trying to fix it himself and called in a computer **expert.**
   a. someone who knows about repairing computers
   b. someone who advertises in newspapers and on television
   c. one of Wei's friends
   d. someone whose computer has also crashed

7. The workers wanted better working conditions. They decided to ask their **employer** to provide a lunch area.
   a. children
   b. boss
   c. bank manager
   d. teacher

8. Almost all of the Europeans who came to America in the early days **settled** along the northeast coast.
   a. looked at the land
   b. moved in and stayed
   c. explored
   d. relocated

9. Why aren't they here yet? Why haven't they arrived? It was almost the **identical** question.
   a. the same
   b. another
   c. the opposite
   d. the following

10. During the long train journey, Max sat opposite an old woman who was knitting. As the knitting **gradually** grew longer, he realized the old woman was knitting a sweater.
    a. all of a sudden
    b. in a flash
    c. little by little
    d. quickly

11. The building was private property. Someone had placed fences around the outside to **prevent** strangers from entering.
    a. stop   b. permit   c. allow   d. check in

12. That island is completely isolated. The nearest island is ten miles distant and the **mainland** is about fifty miles away.
    a. the nearest big island
    b. inhabited land
    c. land with a pier
    d. land mass

13. Most of Iran is situated on a huge **plateau.** The high flat land is cold in winter and hot in summer.
    a. high plain
    b. desert region
    c mountains
    d. flat marshy area

14. His sister was a gifted musician. He never **fully** understood her compositions, but was proud of her all the same.
    a. completely   b. rarely   c. careless   d. not empty

15. Most of the people survived the earthquake, but it had damaged the houses and **destroyed** the new civic center.
    a. used   b. restored   c. blown away   d. ruined

The Marie Celeste

LESSON

1

Pre-reading Questions

1. Can you give the names of any well known ships?

2. What is the name of a famous ship that sank?

3. Can you name a story that makes you frightened?

1

The Marie Celeste

There are many stories about the sea. Some are legends and some are true. One of the strangest is a true story about a sailing ship. It remains a **mystery** even today.

5   In 1872 the *Marie Celeste* started on a trip across the Atlantic Ocean with a crew of ten. Some time later, the captain of another ship, the *Dei Gratia,* spotted the *Marie Celeste.* There was something strange about her appearance.

10 The captain called out, but there was no **response.** The *Marie Celeste* seemed **deserted.**

response ≠ question

When the captain rowed over to **inspect** the ship, no one came to meet him. He knew something was wrong, but there were no signs

15 of violence. Nothing was missing and there was no **damage** to the ship's instruments. Even the lifeboats were still in place. And strangely enough, the **remnants** of a recent meal were on the table. Where was everyone? Did all of the

20 crew decide to jump from the *Marie Celeste* at the same time? Or did a monster come up from the sea onto the ship and take the captain and crew away?

The captain of the *Dei Gratia* looked

25 around for **clues.** The last entry in the *Marie Celeste's* **diary** was ten days earlier, when the ship was more than 400 miles away. However,

diary

the food on the table was only a few days old. If the crew were on the ship a few days ago, why

30 weren't there any later entries in the diary?

No one was able to explain the mystery of the *Marie Celeste,* but the public had many **opinions.** Some thought a giant octopus sucked up the ten members of the **crew**. Others

35 said a whirlwind carried them all away. A few people believed the *Marie Celeste* was under a **curse,** because it sank on a later voyage. Now that the *Marie Celeste* lies somewhere at the bottom of the ocean, no one can ever **solve** the

40 mystery.

crew

find the answer

A Vocabulary

Put the right word in the blanks. The sentences are from the text.

crew	clues	opinions	deserted
diary	inspect	mystery	damage
remnants	curse	solve	response

1. Nothing was missing and there was no _____ to the ship's instruments.
2 A few people believed the *Marie Celeste* was under a _____, because it sank on a later voyage.
3. The *Marie Celeste* seemed _____.
4. Now that the *Marie Celeste* lies somewhere at the bottom of the ocean, no one can ever _____ the mystery.
5. When the captain rowed over to _____ the ship, no one came to meet him.
6. No one was able to explain the mystery of the *Marie Celeste,* but the public had many _____.
7. And strangely enough, the _____ of a recent meal were on the table.
8. It remains a _____ even today.

9. The captain called out, but there was no _____.
10. The last entry in the *Marie Celeste's* _____ was ten days earlier, when the ship was more than 400 miles away.
11. The captain of the *Dei Gratia* looked around for _____.
12. Some thought a giant octopus sucked up the ten members of the _____.

B Vocabulary (new context)

Put the right word in the blanks.

inspect	damage	response	diary
deserted	clues	remnants	solve
opinions	crew	curse	mystery

1. He looked at the _____ to his car. It was worse than he thought.
2. The captain and _____ were happy the voyage was over.
3. There was no _____ to the teacher's question. The class was silent.
4. Many young people keep a _____ in which they write down all their secrets.
5. An officer came to _____ the burned house. He reported the fire was an accident.
6. Although the house seemed _____, Sally was sure someone lived there.
7. There were many _____ about the cause of the war.
8. The school kids tried to _____ the puzzle of the third footprint.
9. It was a _____. Someone entered a locked room and stole the jewels.
10. There were some _____ of material in the box. She decided to start on a patchwork quilt.
11. The only _____ to the murder were a railway ticket and a locker key.
12. That family is under a _____. Three of their children died in less than a year.

C Vocabulary Review

Put the right word in the blanks.

label	series	predict	artificial
vegetarians	supports	substitute	hormones
weapons	experiment	athletes	focus

1. _____ say they are healthier not eating meat.
2. Make sure it says "tomatoes" on the _____ before you open the can.
3. Their regular goalkeeper was sick, so the school provided a _____.
4. She heard a _____ of shots out in the fields and wondered if the hunters were already there.
5. "Mom _____ me," Rena told her father defiantly. "She says I can have my ears pierced."
6. The weather forecasters _____ heavy rain and strong winds for this afternoon.
7. Scientists _____ with animals to find out about human diseases.
8. The _____ the soldiers used were mainly knives and guns.
9. People who take sports seriously and play well are called _____.
10. Professional football teams play on _____ grass. It's a bright green plastic.
11. The farmer added _____ to the hens' feed to make them start laying eggs sooner.
12. After that virus killed so many people, scientists started to _____ on where it originated.

D Comprehension: Multiple Choice

Put a circle around the letter of the best answer.

1. The name of the ship that disappeared was the _____.
   a. *Dei Gratia*   c.   *Marie Celeste*
   b. The name remained a mystery.   d.   *Marie Azores*

2. The *Marie Celeste* was sailing in the _____ Ocean.
   a. Atlantic
   b. Indian
   c. Pacific
   d. Japanese

3. The story takes place in the year _____.
   a. The year is not given.
   b. 1880
   c. 1782
   d. 1872

4. The captain who discovered the *Marie Celeste* was called

   _____.

   a. Michael
   b. The captain's name is not given.
   c. Captain Nicolai
   d. Dei Gratia

5. There were the remnants of a recent _____.
   a. fight
   b. death
   c. whirlwind
   d. meal

6. The last entry in the diary was _____ days ago.
   a. four
   b. seven
   c. 400
   d. ten

7. The *Marie Celeste* had traveled more than _____ miles since the last entry in the diary.
   a. 400
   b. 200
   c. ten
   d. seven

8. The food on the table was only _____ old.
   a. a few hours
   b. seven days
   c. a few days
   d. some days

9. The mystery of the *Marie Celeste* was _____ solved.
   a. probably
   b. never
   c. finally
   d. at last

E Questions

The asterisk (*) means you have to think of the answer. You cannot find it in the text.

1. What sort of a ship was the *Marie Celeste?*

2. How many crew members did the *Marie Celeste* have when she started? How many when she was discovered?
3. Where was she sailing?
4. Was this less than a century ago? More than a century ago? What was the date?
5. Who first knew that there was something wrong with the *Marie Celeste?*
6. Why did the captain row over to inspect the *Marie Celeste?*
7. When was the last entry in the diary, and when was the last meal eaten?
8. What is strange about these last two facts?
9. How far had the ship traveled in ten days?
10. Was anyone able to explain the mystery of the *Marie Celeste?*
*11. What's your theory about the *Marie Celeste?*
12. What happened to the *Marie Celeste* on a later voyage?

F Main Ideas

Which is the main idea of this chapter? Choose one.

1. One of the unexplained mysteries of the sea is the disappearance of the captain and crew from the *Marie Celeste.*
2. The sea is full of unexplained mysteries, and that's why it's dangerous to travel by ship.
3. The *Marie Celeste* traveled for 400 miles without a captain and crew.

The Poltergeist of Rosenheim

LESSON

2

Pre-reading Questions

1. Is the picture old or recent? How can you tell?
2. What do you think is happening?
3. If you were one of the people in the picture, how would you feel?

2

The Poltergeist of Rosenheim

Imagine you are in a room by yourself. Suddenly a cup flies past you and **shatters** against the wall. When this happens, some people say you may be in the company of a "poltergeist." It's a name used to explain strange happenings. A poltergeist smashes dishes and makes loud noises. An **invisible** person seems to be pushing and throwing objects around. Is there a teenager in the house? Some people believe a poltergeist **operates** only when young people are near.

In 1967, a lawyer in the German town of Rosenheim had some trouble at his office. Strange things were happening. Light bulbs **exploded** for no reason. The electrical equipment stopped operating. Telephones rang all the time, but when the lawyer answered, no one was there. There were thousands of calls from the lawyer's office, but no one in the office was making them. The bills were **outrageous,** and the lawyer was worried.

He asked technical **experts** for help. They were **amazed** when they saw drawers opening and heavy filing cabinets moving by themselves. Then they discovered that the poltergeist first appeared when a nineteen-year-old girl,

shatters

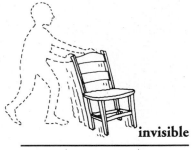

invisible

exploded

very surprised

Anne-Marie, started to work at the office. They
also noticed that when Anne-Marie was not at
work, things were normal.

30   The young girl didn't know that she was
the **cause** of the strange happenings. She had
no desire to upset her **employer**. But when she   employer = boss
left her job, the poltergeist left too.

Scientists who study the **supernatural** said
35 no one was playing tricks. Anne-Marie just
seemed to have some sort of **unusual** power. No
one was ever able to explain what happened.

A Vocabulary

Put the right word in the blanks. The sentences are from the text.

unusual	employer	invisible	operates
cause	amazed	outrageous	exploded
experts	shatters	supernatural	imagine

1. They were _____ when they saw drawers opening and
    heavy filing cabinets moving by themselves.
2. _____ you are in a room by yourself.
3. Scientists who study the _____ said no one was playing
    tricks.
4. The bills were _____, and the lawyer was worried.
5. Some people believe a poltergeist _____ only when
    young people are near.
6. Light bulbs _____ for no reason.
7. Suddenly a cup flies past you and _____ against the wall.
8. An _____ person seems to be pushing and throwing
    objects around.
9. The young girl didn't know that she was the _____ of
    the strange happenings.
10. Anne-Marie just seemed to have some sort of _____
    power.
11. He asked technical _____ for help.
12. She had no desire to upset her _____.

B Vocabulary (new context)

Put the right word in the blanks.

shatters	outrageous	imagine	exploded
unusual	supernatural	employer	cause
amazed	expert	invisible	operates

1. Witches and vampires are _____ beings with strange powers.
2. The _____ gave all his workers extra time off for the holidays.
3. The white Arctic hare is almost _____ in the snowy winters of Alaska.
4. The firecracker _____ with a loud bang, waking the neighbors.
5. Smoking is a leading _____ of lung cancer.
6. When you drop a glass, it usually _____ into many pieces.
7. At eleven Ella is already such a computer _____ that adults come to her with their problems.
8. "_____ ! I'm not paying that amount for a pair of jeans," cried Arnie.
9. She was _____ that he'd even consider playing tennis on such a rainy day.
10. Instead of the popular French folk song, she chose to sing a more _____ piece by a Hungarian composer.
11. Can you _____ how happy I was! I hadn't seen my friends in months!
12. The ferry service only _____ during the summer months when there are plenty of visitors.

C Vocabulary Review

Match the words that mean the same. The first one is done for you.

Column A

1. remnants _____*j*_____
2. solve _____
3. suddenly _____

Column B

a. found
b. something unexplained
c. all at once

Column A		Column B
4. discovered	_____	d. agreeable
5. appeared	_____	e. abandoned
6. fiction	_____	f. came into sight
7. deserted	_____	g. an imaginary story
8. curse	_____	h. reply
9. inspect	_____	i. invisible
10. pleasant	_____	j. remains
11. mystery	_____	k. unusual
12. objects	_____	l. things
13. strange	_____	m. to wish harm
14. response	_____	n. explain
		o. look at carefully

D Comprehension: Sequence

Number these sentences in the correct order. The first one is done for you.

_____ When Anne-Marie left her job, the poltergeist left too.

_____ The bills were enormous.

_____ The experts arrived, and were amazed when they saw the strange happenings.

___1___ This story is about the poltergeist of Rosenheim.

_____ In 1967, strange things started to happen in a lawyer's office.

_____ Besides light bulbs exploding, thousands of telephones calls were made.

_____ The lawyer asked technical experts to help him.

_____ A fitting end to this story is to add that no one has been able to explain this mystery.

_____ First, the experts discovered that the poltergeist first appeared when a young girl, Anne-Marie, started work at the office.

_____ Then they noticed that when she was absent, things were normal.

_____ Light bulbs exploded for no reason.

E Questions

The asterisk (*) means you have to think of the answer. You cannot find it in the text.

1. Did people ever see the poltergeist of Rosenheim?
2. What are some of the actions of a poltergeist?
3. In what country is Rosenheim?
4. Why did the lawyer ask experts to help him?
5. Can you name three strange things that happened in the lawyer's office?
6. Were the telephone bills normal?
7. Why were the technical experts amazed?
8. When did the poltergeist of Rosenheim first appear?
9. When Anne-Marie was not at work, were things normal?
10. Did she want to upset her employer?
11. How did the experts explain the strange happenings?
*12. What do you think happened?

F Main Ideas

Which is the main idea of this chapter? Choose one.

1. Experts weren't able to explain the mysterious happenings of Rosenheim.
2. The lawyer was puzzled over the mysterious happenings.
3. The poltergeist disappeared when Anne-Marie left the office.

The Roanoke Settlement

LESSON

3

Pre-reading Questions

1. How can you tell this man is an explorer?

2. Can you name some great explorers?

3. This portrait is about 400 years old. What's the oldest photo in your family?

The Roanoke Settlement

Only a few Europeans lived in North America in the 1500s. Most of them **settled** along the northeast coast. In 1587, a small group of one hundred people decided to go
5 south. They moved to the small island of Roanoke. That area later became part of the state of North Carolina.

Unfortunately, the Roanoke settlers weren't well prepared. They had to ration their food for
10 winter, and there wasn't enough grain for future crops. Their leader, Captain White, decided to sail back to England to get fresh **provisions.** However, there was a war in Europe, and three years passed before he returned to North America.

15 When Captain White finally sailed back to Roanoke in 1590, he was **eager** to see the settlers. He looked out from his ship as it came into port, but no one was there to meet him. The settlement was deserted. There were no signs of
20 life. The Roanoke settlers had simply **vanished.**

No one knows why they disappeared. Many people thought **hostile** tribes of Native Americans killed them, but there were no signs of a fight. Some thought that the settlers died
25 from hunger or disease, but they couldn't explain the **absence** of bodies.

made a home

provisions

disappeared

hostile ≠ friendly

Much later, more settlers came to North Carolina. One of them was out riding one day. He came across a Native American group called the Lumbee. They were unusual looking in **com-parison** with the other black-haired, brown-eyed Native Americans in the north. Some Lumbee had blonde hair and gray eyes. Then he listened to their speech and almost fell off his horse. They seemed to be speaking an odd kind of English!

He asked where they were from. None of them knew, but said their grandparents "talked from a book." He guessed it meant that their **ancestors** were able to read. As he rode back home he asked himself a question. Were the Lumbee Indians the **descendants** of the Roanoke settlers?

People are still asking the **identical** question. Because there are no written **records,** we can't be certain. However, there is one interesting fact. Today, some of the Lumbee people have names like Sampson, Dare, and Cooper. They are identical to those of the vanished settlers of Roanoke Island.

ancestors

the same

◼️ A ◼️ Vocabulary

Put the right word in the blanks. The sentences are from the text.

eager	identical	descendants	provisions
vanished	records	comparison	ancestors
settled	unfortunately	hostile	absence

1. Were the Lumbee Indians the _____ of the Roanoke settlers?
2. The Roanoke settlers had simply _____.
3. Most of them _____ along the northeast coast.
4. They were unusual looking in _____ with the other black-haired, brown-eyed Native Americans in the north.

5. Some thought that the settlers died from hunger or disease, but they couldn't explain the _____ of bodies.

6. Because there are no written _____, we can't be certain.

7. He guessed it meant that their _____ were able to read.

8. When Captain White finally sailed back to Roanoke in 1590, he was _____ to see the settlers.

9. Many people thought _____ tribes of Native Americans killed them, but there were no signs of a fight.

10. People are still asking the _____ question.

11. _____, the Roanoke settlers weren't well prepared.

12. Their leader, Captain White, decided to sail back to England to get fresh _____.

B Vocabulary (new context)

Put the right word in the blanks.

unfortunately	settled	descendants	identical
ancestors	provisions	eager	comparison
records	vanished	absence	hostile

1. The campers were out of food. Most of their _____ were gone.

2. They say _____ makes the heart grow fonder. But Billy found a new girlfriend two weeks after he left town.

3. Most of the guests _____ after supper. I think they only came for the food.

4. In _____ with last year, this year's profits are better.

5. _____, she left early and didn't hear the announcement that she'd won the award.

6. The Allens were _____ to their neighbors. They showed it by making a noise late at night and throwing garbage over the fence.

7. Of course the two girls look the same. They're _____ twins.

8. The Hansens live in that house. They are the _____ of the people who first came to our town 100 years ago.

9. In the early days, most Eastern European immigrants to the United States _____ in big cities.

10. "I'm _____ to hear what you've been doing in my absence," said Jenny. "Have you been to the movies? Did you finish your test?"

11. My _____ were a mixture of Greek and Russian, so that's why I speak Greek with a Russian accent.

12. Today, most business _____ are kept in computers. There's not much need for filing cabinets any more.

C Vocabulary Review

Put the right word in the blanks.

outrageous   leaked   members   clues
imagine   operates   unusual   employer
experts   damage   tribes   causes

1. Her fountain pen _____ ink all over the floor.

2. "Just _____ that we're in Paris," suggested Chris. "I'm at an outdoor cafe drinking coffee and looking across at the Eiffel Tower. What are you imagining?"

3. My _____ is Mrs. Phillips of First Bank. She's my boss.

4. Bernard is one of the _____ of the field hockey team.

5. They were _____ in tropical plants after living in Hawaii for five years.

6. That advertising claim is _____! No vitamin can make you younger.

7. He _____ that complicated fork lift.

8. It's very _____ to see horses in big cities today, but 100 years ago it was quite common.

9. The _____ caused by the storm was in the millions of dollars.

10. The languages of many Native American _____ are dead, and English is spoken instead.

11. In mystery novels, the detective finds _____. They lead him to the criminal.

12. What are the _____ of unemployment? At a guess, I'd say lack of job-training programs.

D Comprehension: Multiple Choice

Put a circle around the letter of the best answer.

1. When Captain White sailed back to the Roanoke settlement,
   _____ came to meet him.
   a. a tribe of Native Americans   c. a small group
   b. only one person   d. nobody

2. Only a few Europeans lived in North America in the
   _____.
   a. winter   c. 1600s
   b. 1500s   d. 17th century

3. The Roanoke settlers _____ provisions to see them
   through winter.
   a. had enough   c. didn't have enough
   b. had plenty of   d. had lots of

4. Captain White stayed in England for _____.
   a. five years   c. three years
   b. five months   d. a few months

5. The Lumbee tribe spoke an odd kind of _____.
   a. English   c. French
   b. Native American language   d. Spanish dialect

6. A group of about 100 people moved south to what is now the state of
   _____.
   a. South Carolina   c. West Virginia
   b. Virginia   d. North Carolina

7. Captain White couldn't return to Roanoke for three years because there
   was a _____ in Europe.
   a. famine   c. plague
   b. war   d. festival

8. Much later, more settlers moved south and met Native Americans called
   the _____
   a. Roanoke   c. Lumbee
   b. Carolinas   d. Europe

9. Some of the Lumbee names were _____ to those of the vanished Roanoke settlement.
   a. unknown
   b. identical
   c. unfamiliar
   d. limited

E   Questions

The asterisk (*) means you have to think of the answer. You cannot find it in the text.

1. Where did most Europeans settle when they first came to North America?
2. How many people were in the group that moved south?
3. Where did they settle?
4. Why were they called the Roanoke settlers?
*5. "That area later became part of the state of North Carolina." Why wasn't Roanoke part of North Carolina then?
6. Were the Roanoke settlers well prepared for winter?
7. Who decided to sail back to England? Why?
8. How long was he away? What stopped him from coming back?
9. In what year did he come back? What did he see?
10. What was the name of the tribe that spoke an odd sort of English?
11. The Lumbee said their grandparents "talked from a book." What is another way of putting this?
12. What are the names of some of the Lumbee people? What is interesting about those names?

F   Main Ideas

Which is the main idea of this chapter? Choose one.

1. In the late 1500s, the Roanoke settlers vanished, and no one knows for certain where they went.
2. The Lumbee tribe are definitely descendants of the lost Roanoke settlers.
3. The mystery of the Roanoke settlers proves that nothing is really known about the 1500s in America.

The Easter Island Statues

LESSON

4

Pre-reading Questions

1. Are these statues of normal people? Why? Why not?

2. Can you name some islands you'd like to visit?

3. There are several Easter, Christmas and Thursday Islands. Why?

The Easter Island Statues

When the first sailing ship came to Easter Island in 1722, the captain and crew were afraid to land. They saw giants looking down at them from the high cliffs. The giants didn't
5 move, so the ship **gradually** sailed closer. Finally, the sailors realized the giants were only **statues.** These huge carvings have **puzzled** the world ever since. Who made them? How did they get there?

10 Easter Island is a small dot in the South Pacific Ocean. It is hundreds of miles away from the nearest shipping route, and it is one of the most isolated places on earth. The nearest **mainland** is over 2,000 miles away in
15 South America.

The biggest statue on Easter Island is over 60 feet high and weighs over 100 tons. There are hundreds of smaller ones, about 15 feet high. All of the statues are carved from stone
20 and some wear stone hats. Their faces are **solemn** and unsmiling.

Earlier inhabitants of Easter Island carved the statues from the rocks in a volcanic **crater.** Next, they had to move the statues a long dis-
25 tance, in some cases more than ten miles, to **erect** them in their present position.

slowly

statues

large mass of land

solemn

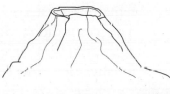

crater

No one knows for certain how the inhabitants **achieved** this very difficult feat. Some scientists say that palm trees grew on Easter Island
30 in the past. They think the inhabitants cut the trees down and placed the heavy statues on the tree trunks. Then groups of seventy or more people rolled the statues to their present locations. Other scientists dispute this **theory**
35 because there are no palm trees on the island today. More importantly, the **actual** purpose of the statues remains a mystery. Some, at least, were probably placed on the cliffs to **prevent** strangers from landing on the island.

prevent ≠ allow

40 The result, however, has been the opposite. **Crowds** of eager people come to gape at the statues. Easter Island is no longer a dot on the map. It has a modern airport and tourists visit from all over the world.

lots of people

A Vocabulary

Put the right word in the blanks. The sentences are from the text.

statues	actual	theory	gradually
mainland	crowds	erect	puzzled
crater	prevent	achieved	solemn

1. The nearest _____ is over 2,000 miles away in South America.
2. These huge carvings have _____ the world ever since.
3. Other scientists dispute this _____ because there are no palm trees on the island today.
4. More importantly, the _____ purpose of the statues remains a mystery.
5. The giants didn't move, so the ship _____ sailed closer.
6. _____ of eager people come to gape at the statues.
7. Finally, the sailors realized the giants were only _____.

8. Next, they had to move the statues a long distance, in some cases more than ten miles, to _____ them in their present position.
9. No one knows for certain how the inhabitants _____ this very difficult feat.
10. Earlier inhabitants of Easter Island carved the statues from the rocks in a volcanic _____.
11. Some, at least, were probably placed on the cliffs to _____ strangers from landing on the island.
12. Their faces are _____ and unsmiling.

B Vocabulary (new context)

Put the right word in the blanks.

achieved	puzzled	crowds	actual
crater	statues	theory	prevent
gradually	mainland	erect	solemn

1. The island was separated from the _____ by a narrow stretch of water.
2. In _____, we know it's better to have eight hours' sleep. In practice, we often make do with five or six.
3. _____ of former kings and queens lined the entrance to the cathedral.
4. There were _____ of noisy fans surrounding the movie star, asking for autographs.
5. Brandi _____ her heart's desire when she passed the entrance exam for Yale.
6. He was _____ about the knocking on the kitchen window until he saw the next-door cat.
7. The _____ wedding took place three days after the date on the invitation.
8. Mrs. Carson's face was _____ when she told her class about the pet mouse's escape, but secretly she was rejoicing.
9. The _____ of the volcano wasn't dead. The villagers expected it to erupt at any moment.
10. In a game called "What's the Time, Mr. Wolf?" the players _____ creep up to the person in front.

11. "I know what! We'll _____ a statue to you," cried the grateful king.

12. What can we do to _____ the birds from returning and eating the fruit?

C Vocabulary Review

Match the words that mean the opposite. The first one is done for you.

Column A   **Column B**

1. eager   ____h____   a. presence
2. vanished   _____   b. fortunately
3. unfortunately _____   c. confident
4. hostile   _____   d. plentiful
5. absence   _____   e. adored
6. afraid   _____   f. careful
7. hated   _____   g. allows
8. careless   _____   h. unwilling
9. earlier   _____   i. friendly
10. probable   _____   j. employee
11. forbids   _____   k. appeared
12. familiar   _____   l. strange
13. scarce   _____   m. later
14. employer   _____   n. unlikely

D Comprehension: True/False/No Information

Write T if the sentence is true. Write F if it is false. Write NI if no information is given.

1. The first ship to arrive at Easter Island was a steam ship.
2. The sailors were afraid to land because they thought there were giants on the island.
3. Sailing closer, the sailors realized that the giants were only statues.
4. Easter Island is very close to the mainland of South America.
5. Easter Island lies in the North Pacific Ocean.
6. There are many huge stone statues on the island.
7. The statues have smiling faces.

8. The present inhabitants of Easter Island carved the statues.
9. There are many volcanos on the island.
10. There are no theories as to how the statues were placed in their present position.
11. No palm trees grow on the island today.
12. The statues were placed on the cliff to welcome tourists.
13. Today, many tourists visit Easter Island to look at the statues.

E Questions

The asterisk (*) means you have to think of the answer. You cannot find it in the text.

1. Is Easter Island large or small?
2. Which ocean is it in?
3. How far away is the nearest mainland?
4. What are the statues of Easter Island made from?
5. How tall is the biggest statue?
6. How much does it weigh?
7. Can you describe the faces of the statues?
8. Where were the rocks for the statues found?
9. How far were some of the statues moved?
10. Did the present inhabitants of Easter Island carve the statues?
11. What is one possible reason why the statues were carved?
*12. Why do you think there is an airport on Easter Island?

F Main Ideas

Which is the main idea of this chapter? Choose one.

1. Long ago, statues were placed on Easter Island by the early inhabitants. Their purpose remains a mystery.
2. The early inhabitants of Easter Island spent years placing the statues in their present positions.
3. Easter Island is now a well known tourist resort.

The Tunguska Fireball

LESSON

5

Pre-reading Questions

1. Are the upper and lower photos connected? How?

2. When some people see a falling star, they cross their fingers and make a wish. Why do you think this is?

3. Can you name some unusual things you might occasionally see in the sky?

The Tunguska Fireball

At night, you can sometimes see a **meteor** if there are no bright lights nearby. We call it a "falling star." Most meteors die as they enter the earth's **atmosphere.** The sun burns them up,
5 even though they are made of rock and metal.

When a meteor hits the earth, it is then called a meteorite. Most are very small. However, occasionally in the past, large meteorites hit the earth and made huge craters.
10 There is a one in Australia and another in Arizona. They are both thousands of years old.

Was a meteorite the cause of the explosion in Tunguska, in central Siberia, in 1908? On June 30 of that year, the inhabitants of the
15 lonely Tungus **plateau** saw a very bright light in the sky. Seconds later, they heard a **tremendous** explosion. As far away as Europe, people saw their night sky **illuminated.** For years afterwards, they talked about the brightness of
20 the sky that night.

Tunguska is so remote that it was twenty years before scientists traveled there to look for the cause of the explosion. Even after all that time, the area was still completely **destroyed.**
25 Trees were black from the explosion and lay flat

meteor

plateau

lit

ruined

on the ground for a twenty-mile **radius.** At first, scientists thought a meteorite was the cause. When they couldn't find a crater, they thought it might be the blast from an early top-secret atomic bomb. Others said it might be a huge ball of fire. A lot of the theories were really just **guesswork.** Newspapers printed **articles** on the fireball of Tunguska. Some **journalists** went further. They wrote about the crash landing of an **alien** space ship.

Years have passed since then, but even today no one can **fully** explain the Tunguska explosion. One recent theory is that a meteor exploded just before it hit the earth's surface. That is why there was no crater like those in Arizona and Australia. However, no one knows for certain, and the explosion in Tunguska remains a mystery.

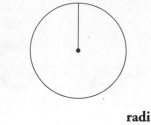

radius

A Vocabulary

Put the right word in the blanks. The sentences are from the text.

alien	destroyed	radius	meteor
atmosphere	articles	journalists	plateau
tremendous	illuminated	guesswork	fully

1. A lot of the theories were really just _____.
2. They wrote about the crash landing of an _____ space ship.
3. Newspapers printed _____ on the fireball of Tunguska.
4. At night, you can sometimes see a _____ if there are no bright lights nearby.
5. On June 30 of that year, the inhabitants of the lonely Tungus _____ saw a very bright light in the sky.
6. As far away as Europe, people saw their night sky _____.
7. Some _____ went further.
8. Even after all that time, the area was still completely _____.
9. Most meteors die when they enter the earth's _____.

10. Seconds later they heard a _____ explosion.
11. Trees were black from the explosion and lay flat on the ground for a twenty-mile _____.
12. Years have passed since then, but even today no one can _____ explain the Tunguska explosion.

B Vocabulary (new context)

Put the right word in the blanks.

destroyed	illuminated	meteor	radius
alien	journalists	plateau	tremendous
guesswork	articles	atmosphere	fully

1. Movies about an encounter with a space _____ are a popular choice with young people.
2. Paris is called the City of Light because many of its historic buildings are _____ at night.
3. I looked up at the night sky and suddenly a _____ flashed past.
4. Teenagers loved the noisy _____ of the cafe.
5. "I don't really know, it's just _____," admitted Melinda.
6. The storm _____ almost every house near the ocean.
7. The _____ gathered around the lawyer as he came out of the courtroom. "What was the verdict?" one asked eagerly.
8. No one _____ understood the professor's theories.
9. The _____ is the line going from the center to the edge of a circle. We learned that in geometry.
10. Newspaper _____ are often written in a hurry.
11. The _____ was high, over 3,000 feet above sea level.
12. The _____ wave caused Julian to fall off his surfboard.

C Vocabulary Review

Underline the word that does not belong.

1. lonely, remote, isolated, solemn
2. motionless, still, unmoving, erect
3. theory, idea, diary, proposal
4. hormones, people, inhabitants, tribe
5. mainland, island, valley, remainder

6. forbid, damage, stop, prevent
7. amazed, solemn, sad, sorrowful
8. got, achieved, inspected, completed
9. legend, story, tale, media

D Comprehension

Put a circle around the letter of the best answer.

1. There are _____ huge craters on the earth's surface that were made by meteorites.
   a. several
   b. no
   c. many
   d. many hundreds of

2. On June 30, 1908, there was a tremendous _____ in Tunguska.
   a. damage
   b. tundra
   c. explosion
   d. mystery

3. The explosion caused a great amount of _____.
   a. damage
   b. smoke
   c. craters
   d. holes

4. Even twenty years later, the area around Tunguska was _____.
   a. completely destroyed
   b. completely inspected
   c. completely restored
   d. completely invisible

5. Tunguska is a remote area of _____.
   a. Alaska
   b. Arizona
   c. Siberia
   d. Australia

6. Meteorites are meteors that _____.
   a. burn up as they enter the earth's atmosphere
   b. hit the earth
   c. sometimes make large craters in the earth's surface
   d. both b and c

7. A plateau is another name for _____.
   a. an area devastated by an explosion
   b. a high flat area
   c. a Siberian dwelling
   d. a compound of ice and metal

8. At first, scientists thought a _____ was the cause of the explosion.
   - a. fireball
   - b. hole
   - c. meteorite
   - d. alien spaceship

E Questions

The asterisk (*) means you have to think of the answer. You cannot find it in the text.

1. What happens to most meteors when they enter the earth's atmosphere?
2. What is a meteor called when it hits the ground?
3. What usually happens when large meteors hit the earth?
4. Where is the Tunguska region?
5. What happened there in 1908?
6. How did people in Europe know that something had happened?
7. Why was it so long before scientists traveled to Tunguska to see what had happened?
8. What was the area like after twenty years?
9. Can you name two possibilities about what happened in Tunguska?
10. What did some journalists write about?
11. Are there any craters in other parts of the world that are caused by meteorites? If so, where are they?
*12. What do you think was the cause of the Tunguska explosion?

F Main Ideas

Which is the main idea of this chapter? Choose one.

1. The Tunguska fireball caused damage that was visible twenty years later.
2. The Tunguska fireball was so powerful that it illuminated the sky in Europe.
3. In 1908 a mysterious explosion occurred in Siberia. No one really knows what happened.

Word Study

A Conjunctions: and/but

We use conjunctions to connect ideas in a sentence. The conjunction "but" shows a contrast between two ideas. The conjunction "and" shows a similarity between two ideas.

Example: I wanted to eat outside, **but** it was raining.
                  I like to travel, **but** no one else in my family does.

Example: I wanted to eat outside, **and** my friends did too.
                  I like to travel, **and** all of my friends do too.

Add the conjunction *and* or *but* to these sentences.

1. The captain expected to find someone on the *Marie Celeste,* _____ no one was there.
2. The last diary entry on the *Marie Celeste* was ten days old, _____ the food was only a few days old.
3. The lifeboats on the *Marie Celeste* were still in place, _____ nothing on the ship was missing.
4. The poltergeist of Rosenheim caused a lot of damage, _____ it didn't hurt anyone.
5. Technical experts studied the strange happenings, _____ they never discovered what caused them.
6. The Roanoke settlers didn't have enough food for the winter, _____ they lacked grain for their future crops.
7. Captain White was eager to see the settlers, _____ no one came to greet him.
8. People thought that the early Roanoke settlers had vanished forever, _____ there are people today who still have the same names.
9. The Easter Island statues are carved from stone, _____ some wear stone hats.
10. The inhabitants of Tunguska saw a brilliant flash, _____ seconds later they heard a tremendous explosion.
11. Trees were still black from the explosion, _____ many of them lay flat on the ground.

B Spelling Review

1. Look at the words below and then answer the questions.

Singular	Plural	Singular	Plural
toy	toys	navy	navies
holiday	holidays	story	stories
day	days	city	cities
delay	delays	party	parties

a. How do you form the plural of a noun that ends in *-y* with a consonant before it?

b. How do you form the plural of a noun that ends in a vowel plus *-y?*

Write the plural form of these nouns.

1. mystery _____
2. donkey _____
3. theory _____
4. army _____
5. tray _____
6. enemy _____
7. diary _____
8. x-ray _____
9. fantasy _____
10. boy _____

C Word Forms

	Verb	Noun	Adjective
1.	respond	response	
2.	desert	desertion	
3.	inspect	inspection	
4.		mystery	mysterious
5.	imagine	imagination	imaginative
6.		accuracy	accurate
7.	compare	comparison	comparable
8.	achieve	achievement	
9.	destroy	destruction	

Put the correct word form in the blanks. Choose a word from Line 1 in Sentence 1, and so on. Use the right verb forms and singular and plural nouns.

1. Who can _____ to that question? What, no _____?

2. The _____ surprised the captain. He knew the work was dangerous, but he didn't expect his next-in-command to _____ him.

3. There is going to be an important _____ tomorrow. I hope everything is ready when the boss comes to _____ the office.

4. There was some _____ story about a ghost wandering in the garden. However, the _____ was eventually explained. It was a white goat.

5. What an _____ that author has! In her last novel, she _____ she lived five hundred years ago in Hungary.

6. The newspaper doesn't have an _____ account of what happened. The neighbors tell the story with more _____ than that.

7. Talking in loud voices, the two mothers _____ their daughters. Mrs. Blanchard said there was no _____ between the two girls. Colette was better at everything and that was that.

8. What is your most important _____? Winning the trophy? Was it difficult to _____?

9. The tornado _____ everything in its path. The _____ was total.

D Regular and Irregular Verbs

Write the past tense of these verbs. Then use the past tense of each verb in a sentence.

1. inspect _____
2. curse _____
3. come up _____
4. settle _____
5. achieve _____

6. come   _____
7. find   _____
8. hit   _____
9. imagine   _____
10. puzzle   _____

E Writing

Choose one or more of these topics and write answers.

1. Which of the five mysteries was the strangest to you? Why?
2. Pretend a member of the crew of the *Marie Celeste* wrote a message, put it in a bottle, and dropped the bottle in the ocean. You just found the bottle with the message. What does the message say?
3. Describe something mysterious—something you have read or heard about.

Video Highlights

©CNN

A Before You Watch

1. You have read about Easter Island. Write T if the sentence below is true. Write F if it is not true.

_____ a. Easter Island is one of the most remote islands in the world.
_____ b. The island is famous for its mysterious paintings.
_____ c. Some of the statues on Easter Island are over 60 feet tall.
_____ d. Easter Island is one of the largest islands in the world.

2. These words will help you understand the video. Read the words and their definitions.

a. puzzles: mysteries
b. *moai:* the Easter Island name for its famous statues
c. contact: to get in touch with someone
d. linger: to remain for a long time

Now choose one of the words above for each of these sentences. You will hear similar sentences in the video.

a. The _____ were built by the original inhabitants.
b. The original inhabitants of Easter Island were later almost wiped out by _____ with North American adventurers and Latin American slave traders.

c. Many questions _____ with visitors to Easter Island.

d. Easter Island is one of the planet's greatest archeological _____.

1. There are some interesting facts in this video. As you watch, fill in the blanks in the sentences with some of the numbers from the list below.

hundreds	3,000	fifty-five	1914	111
twenty	sixty	1870s	thousands	15,000

a. Some statues weigh _____ of tons.

b. They are as much as _____ meters, or _____ feet high.

c. Tourism can have a downside for the island's _____ inhabitants.

d. By the _____ only _____ Easter Islanders remained.

2. At the end of the video, you will hear three questions. They are written below, but not in the correct order. Put them in order by writing 1, 2, 3, in the spaces at the beginning of the question.

_____ How did they chisel the statues in the quarry on the side of the volcano?

_____ Where did the first Easter Islanders come from?

_____ How did they move them and why did they do it?

C After You Watch

2. The map on the next page is of Easter Island.

a. Draw an arrow pointing in the direction of the mainland.

b. Write in "Pacific Ocean" and "Easter Island" on the appropriate lines on the map.

c. Moto Nui is an island off Easter Island's southwestern tip. Make a cross where it is on the map.

d. In one of the four circles on the map, write an *N* for north.
e. Draw a triangle connecting the three main volcanoes of Ranu Kau, Maunga Terevaka, and Katiki.
f. The original inhabitants of Easter Island made the statues from huge stones lying near the volcanic crater at Rano Raraku. Then they pulled the statues to Vinapu, almost ten miles away. Draw a line from one place to the other.

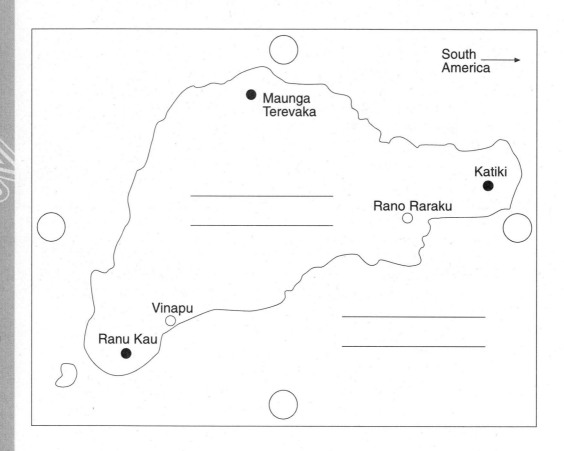

Activity Page

A. Look at the newspaper headline at the left, then use items from the squares below to make up your own headlines. You can use verbs from your textbook: discovers, destroys, puzzles, shatters, amazes, vanishes, captures, knocks out.

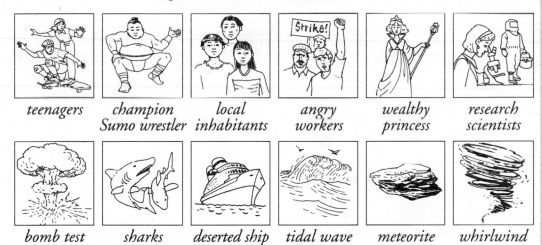

| teenagers | champion Sumo wrestler | local inhabitants | angry workers | wealthy princess | research scientists |

| bomb test | sharks | deserted ship | tidal wave | meteorite | whirlwind |

B. A baby-sitter was in charge of a small boy, Sammy. They were having a snack in the kitchen. She left the room to answer the phone. When she came back she saw that Sammy had damaged 18 items. Work with a partner to find them. You can use the verbs below.

Example: Sammy tore the curtains. He cut the . . . .

damaged   shattered
removed   crushed
opened   broke
emptied   tore
burned   undid
knocked over   destroyed
dirtied   cut
locked   dropped
unrolled   flooded
smashed   wrote

161

Dictionary Page

Informal Usage

Often a word has two uses, one for formal speech and writing, and the other for everyday or informal speech. Your dictionary indicates whether the word has an *informal* meaning.

1. Read the dictionary entries below, then circle the number of the informal entry. The first one is done for you.

broke /broʊk/
1 *past tense of* break
② **broke** *adjective informal*
without money: *I am broke.*

neat /nit/ *adjective*
1 in good order, *(synonym)* tidy: *His house is always neat and clean.*
2 skillfully done: *a neat way of saying something*
3 *informal* great, wonderful: *We had a neat time at the party.* —*adverb* **neatly;** —*noun* **neatness.**

lot /lɑt/ *noun*
1 a piece of land: *We own a small lot next to our house.*
2 *(no plural)* one's condition in life: *It was his lot to become a priest.*
3 *informal* **a lot (of)** or **lots (of):** a large amount or number: *I like her a lot.||He has lots of money, problems, etc.*

nut /nʌt/ *noun*
1 a fruit with a hard shell or its seed: *a candy made from fruit and nuts*
2 *informal* a person who seems very odd or crazy: *Stop acting like a nut!*
3 a small piece of metal with a hole in the middle used with a bolt.

kid /kɪd/ *noun*
1 *informal* a child
2 a young goat

noodle /ˈnudl/ *noun*
1 a long, narrow or wide flat strip of pasta made from a mixture of flour, egg, and water: *Boil the noodles first.*
2 *informal* head: *You can figure it out; just use your noodle!*

2. Decide whether the words in bold are used formally or informally. Put a check in the appropriate column.

	formal	informal
a. I'm so **broke** I can't afford to buy lunch.	_____	_____
b. Fruit cake always contains raisins and **nuts.**	_____	_____
c. That was a really **neat** piece of music.	_____	_____
d. What's the name of your **kid** brother?	_____	_____

e. Julio's made **a lot of** enemies. _____ _____

f. She always kept her room **neat** and tidy. _____ _____

3. **Write the correct formal word in the sentences below.**

   a. My brother John is only a _____. (child, kid, goat)

   b. He always dresses like some _____. (crazy person, nut, noodle)

   c. That cake's got _____ cream in it. (a large amount of, a lot of, heaps of)

   d. Don't be silly! Have you lost your _____? (head, noodle, beans)

   e. Your sister's really _____. (cool, neat, nice)

   f. I'm _____. My purse is empty. (without money, broke, bust)

Business

Context Clues

Choose the lettered answer that means the same as the words in bold.

1. What a **contrast** the two brothers were. Charles is on the debating team. He's tall and thin and very studious. Jake is the sports lover. He's short and stodgy and plays hockey.
   a. The two brothers are very alike.
   b. The two brothers are very different.
   c. The two brothers are sports fans.
   d. The two brothers have many interests.

2. The priest insisted that the decorators paint the walls in white. To her, white was a **symbol** of purity.
   a. theory   c. product
   b. sign   d. article

3. "My **precious** little doggie," she said, patting the dog's head. "I don't know what I'd do without you."
   a. worthless, without value   c. valuable, dear
   b. individual or alone   d. replaced by another

4. Although he came to Canada as a small boy, he always felt himself to be a **foreigner.** It wasn't until he moved to a big city that he felt at home.
   a. journalist   c. outsider
   b. Canadian   d. German

5. While Jan was asking for directions in very bad French, Byron pointed to the map and then to the mountains with a puzzled look on his face. The villager understood. Byron's **gestures** were easier to understand than Jan's speech.
   a. ask for directions in a foreign language
   b. to whisper with the hand over the mouth
   c. make movements of the hands or head
   d. question someone without speaking

6. The new owners **restored** the old house from top to bottom. They replaced the top floor, then painted everything in the original colors.
   a. sold the house   c. painted the walls
   b. made the house look like new   d. swept the floors

7. It was so **typical** of Paul. On the day of the exam he forgot his books, he forgot what room the exam was in, and he forgot his writing materials. He's always forgetting things.
   a. Paul is very forgetful.
   b. It's just like Paul to behave in that way.
   c. Paul will probably fail in his exam.
   d. Paul needs to write notes to remember things.

8. Tell me some of the **customs** of your country. For example, are there any unusual ways of greeting people? Do you have special foods? What are your biggest feast days?
   a. special thoughts   c. special behavior
   b. special opinions   d. special answers

9. The **theme** of the play was one of divorced or separated couples coming together again.
   a. acting   c. origin
   b. central idea   d. leading actors

10. He's very good at **imitating** people. I've seen him do politicians and movie actors, but he's best at ordinary people.
    a. making friends with   c. copying the actions of
    b. signing agreements with d. giving money to

11. Business people often take their **clients** out to lunch. It's a good idea because they get to know each other better, and it makes the clients feel valued.
    a. customers   c. wives
    b. friends   d. contracts

12. That poster is part of the **campaign** to abolish drunken driving. Have you seen the television commercials?
    a. an effort or idea to change something
    b. money from a large company
    c. the ideas of a political party
    d. prison sentences for drunken drivers

13. What an **insult!** When I greeted him he walked past me as if he didn't know me.
    a. stupid mistake   c. unkind action or remark
    b. reply or response   d. funny remark

14. The **items** we are going to talk about today are Cash Flow, Contracts and Mass Marketing. We'll start with item one: Cash Flow.
    a. possibilities, chances
    b. arguments or discussions
    c. things listed, topics
    d. funny remarks, jokes

15. The airline pilot used **automatic** controls to guide him to the airport.
    a. The controls operated mechanically.
    b. The pilot needed the ground crew to help him.
    c. The pilot used a telephone to ask for help.
    d. The co-pilot controlled the plane.

The History of Money

LESSON

1

Pre-reading Questions

1. How can you tell the money is from diffcrent countries?

2. Why do coins come in different sizes?

3. Why do you think we have paper money?

1

The History of Money

Today, our **currency** is a mixture of coins and paper money. But it wasn't always that way. Before metal coins and paper **bills** existed, people used a lot of unusual things to buy what they needed. In one part of the world, for example, people used sharks' teeth for money. In some places, brightly colored feathers and rare seashells were money. People in one area even used the bristles from elephants' tails for money.

No one knows for sure when people started using metal coins for money. **Archeologists** have found coins dating from 600 B.C., so we know they have been around for a long time. At first, people used **precious** metals, such as gold and silver, to make coins. They stamped the figure of a person or animal on each coin to **indicate** its value.

In the 1200s, people in China used **iron** coins for their currency. These coins weren't worth very much, so people had to use a lot of them to make their **purchases.** Because it was inconvenient to carry around a large number of heavy iron coins, the government started printing paper **receipts.** People took these receipts to banks and **traded** them in for coins. This is the first example we have of paper money.

bills   **coins**

people who study the past

show

receipts

Today, most countries use a mixture of coins and paper bills for their currency. In the United States, the paper bills are all the same
30 size and color. For example, the one-dollar bill is the same size and color as the one-hundred-dollar bill. In many other countries, the bills come in **various** sizes and colors. The smaller sized bills are worth less money. This makes it
35 easier for people to tell the value of their money at a glance. All these facts make the history of money a **fascinating** study.

Below are some **trivia** points about money.   unimportant details

*   Feathers were the lightest money ever.
40   They were used on the Pacific island of Santa Cruz.

*   Stones were the heaviest money ever. They were used on the Pacific island of Yap. Some weighed over 500 pounds.

45 *   The smallest money ever used was in Greece. The coins were made of metal, but smaller than an apple seed.

A Vocabulary

Put the right word in the blanks. The sentences are from the text.

precious	bills	various	indicate
currency	receipts	purchases	trivia
fascinating	archeologists	traded	iron

1. People took these receipts to banks and _____ them in for coins.
2. Below are some ____ _____ points about money.
3. In the 1200s, people in China used _____ coins for their currency.

4. They stamped the figure of a person or animal on each coin to
   _____ its value.
5. In many other countries, the bills come in _____ sizes
   and colors.
6. At first, people used _____ metals, such as gold and silver, to make coins.
7. Today, our _____ is a mixture of coins and paper money.
8. These coins weren't worth very much, so people had to use a lot of them
   to make their _____.
9. Because it was inconvenient to carry around a large number of heavy
   iron coins, the government started printing paper _____.
10. _____ have found coins dating from 600 B.C., so we
    know they have been around for a long time.
11. All these facts make the history of money a _____ study.
12. Before metal coins and paper _____ existed, people used
    a lot of unusual things to buy what they needed.

B Vocabulary (new context)

Put the right word in the blanks.

trivia	fascinating	iron	archeologists
various	indicate	currency	precious
traded	bills	receipts	purchases

1. Each country has its own _____. In Mexico, it's the peso,
   and in Japan, it's the yen.
2. After they'd scraped away the dirt, the _____ saw the
   pattern on the vase.
3. My friends are more _____ to me than the most valuable
   jewels.
4. She spent most of her spare time taking photographs. It was a
   _____ hobby.
5. The cashier will give you two separate _____ when you
   pay for those two articles.
6. _____ is used in making tools, machinery and other
   strong items.
7. When we returned from the shops, Rita put her _____
   on the table.

8. Dollar _____ get worn after a few years, even though they're made from very strong paper.

9. Bill entered a _____ contest. He won when he was able to recite all the Oscar winners from the movies of 1972.

10. He was an actor in his early life, then had _____ other careers until he retired.

11. Paul _____ his hockey sticks for his friend's skates. I think they're both happy.

12. If you can _____ what time you're leaving, then I can suggest what train to catch.

C Vocabulary Review

Put the right word in the blanks.

gradually	mainland	illuminated	puzzled
fully	radius	destroyed	atmosphere
crowds	prevent	actual	articles

1. I think the _____ cost was much higher. The first price was just guesswork.

2. There are always _____ at film premieres. They come to see their favorite stars arrive.

3. It was _____ a moment before she realized that the train had gone, and there wouldn't be another for three hours.

4. "Find the _____ of the circle and double it. Then you'll have the diameter," the teacher told them.

5. There are several _____ about the crisis in today's newspapers.

6. As they climbed the mountain, the summit _____ appeared.

7. "Everyone ready? We're approaching the _____!" shouted the captain to his crew.

8. That new factory is spoiling the _____ of our quiet village.

9. The lights of the houses _____ the dark winter night.

10. Chris was lucky to escape without being hurt. His car was

_____ .

11. That high fence is to _____ thieves from entering.

12. We were _____ by the lack of mail until we realized there was a postal strike.

D Comprehension: Multiple Choice

Put a circle around the letter of the best answer.

1. In China in the 1200s, coins were made from _____.
   a. gold
   b. copper
   c. silver
   d. iron

2. Archeologists have found coins dating from about _____.
   a. 6000 B.C.
   b. 1600 B.C.
   c. 600 B.C.
   d. 1000 B.C.

3. In most countries, the _____ is a mixture of paper and coins.
   a. dollar
   b. currency
   c. precious metal
   d. receipt

4. Traders in China used iron coins, which they traded at _____ for paper money.
   a. banks
   b. teahouses
   c. warehouses
   d. market places

5. Archeologists are people who study the _____.
   a. present
   b. ways people trade
   c. future
   d. past

6. The Chinese started to use _____ instead of carrying around heavy iron coins.
   a. sharks' teeth
   b. gold and silver
   c. receipts
   d. dollars

7. _____ were the lightest money ever.
   a. sharks' teeth
   b. feathers
   c. seashells
   d. stones

8. _____ were the heaviest money ever.
   a. sharks' teeth
   b. feathers
   c. seashells
   d. stones

9. Some of the stone money weighed over _____ pounds.
   a. 500
   b. 60
   c. 600
   d. 5000

10. The smallest money ever was used in _____.
    a. Greece
    b. China
    c. Italy
    d. The Pacific Islands

11. The smallest coins ever were about the size of _____.
    a. a postage stamp
    b. an apple core
    c. an apple seed
    d. a seashell

12. The bills of other countries come in _____ sizes and colors.
    a. the same
    b. various
    c. inconvenient
    d. identical

E Questions

The asterisk (*) means you have to think of the answer. You cannot find it in the text.

1. What are some of the things people used before there was money?
*2. Why did they use them?
3. Do we know for certain when metal coins were first used?
4. What is the date of the earliest coins?
5. What metal were the first coins made from?
*6. How do most countries indicate the value of coins today?
7. What metal were Chinese coins made from in the 1200s?
8. What country made the first paper money?
9. Why did they make paper money?
10. Where did the people take the receipts?
11. Are paper bills the same size and shape in the United States?
12. Are bills the same size and shape in other countries?

F Main Ideas

Which is the main idea of this chapter? Choose one.

1. In the early days, many unusual things were used as money.
2. Paper currency started in China in the 1200s.
3. Coins and paper gradually replaced shells and sharks' teeth of early money.

Mass Marketing:
The Coca-Cola® Story

LESSON

2

Pre-reading Questions

1. Why is Coca-Cola so easy to recognize?

2. Where do you see Coca-Cola advertisements today?

3. If you're in a foreign country and can't speak the language, why do advertisements like these help?

Mass Marketing:
The Coca-Cola® Story

In the 1880s, people drank John Pemberton's tonic to cure headaches. It wasn't a very popular drink, and he sold only about a dozen bottles a day. That's why Pemberton was willing to sell the
5 rights to his medicinal drink. The buyer, Asa Griggs Candler, paid just $2,300 for the rights to Coca-Cola. Today Coca-Cola is worth over $2,470,000,000. It controls 50% of the world market in soft drinks.

10 How did Coca-Cola become so popular? One answer is that Asa Candler was a very clever businessman. He was one of the first people to use **mass-marketing** techniques. One of the most important things he did was to
15 make his product **unique.** When he bought the rights to Coca-Cola, it was sold in ordinary bottles. It looked like every other drink on the market. To make Coca-Cola look different, Candler **modernized** the bottles. He also
20 designed an eye-catching **logo** for his product. When other companies tried to **imitate** Coca-Cola's name, Candler took them to court.

In addition to the unique bottle and logo, Candler spent a lot of time and money **pro-**
25 **moting** his product. He used advertising to

selling a product in very large quantities

logo

create a powerful **image** of Coca-Cola in the   picture
minds of his customers. He gave away free
samples of Coke. He **advertised** Coca-Cola in
the newspaper, on outdoor posters, and by
30 painting the logo on walls and barns. He put
the name of his drink on pencils, serving
trays, Japanese fans, matches and many other
things and then gave them away. By 1902,
Coca-Cola was the best known product in the
35 United States.

Candler was also able to develop memorable **themes** for his advertisements. For the
first time, famous sports figures **portrayed**   showed
Coca-Cola as a refreshing drink for ordinary
40 people. There were many advertising **campaigns.** They included catchy slogans such as
"The Pause That Refreshes."

Today, mass marketing is used all over the
world, but the **manufacturers** of Coke were   makers
45 the first. It remains the most popular soft
drink ever.

Some trivia points.

• Coca-Cola is sold in more than 195
countries around the world.

50 • People ask for a Coke in 80 different
languages.

• Over 700,000,000 people drink a Coke
every day.

A Vocabulary

Put the right word in the blanks. The sentences are from the text.

modernized	imitate	image	advertised
promoting	themes	mass-marketing	unique
logo	portrayed	campaigns	manufacturers

1. When other companies tried to _____ Coca-Cola's name, Candler took them to court.
2. He was one of the first people to use _____ techniques.
3. In addition to the unique bottle and logo, Candler spent a lot of time and money _____ his product.
4. He _____ Coca-Cola in the newspaper, on outdoor posters, and by painting the logo on walls and barns.
5. For the first time, famous sports figures _____ Coca-Cola as a refreshing drink for ordinary people.
6. Today mass marketing is used all over the world, but the _____ of Coke were the first.
7. He also designed an eye-catching _____ for his product.
8. One of the most important things he did was to make his product _____.
9. There were many advertising _____.
10. Candler was also able to develop memorable _____ for his advertisements.
11. He used advertising to create a powerful _____ of Coca-Cola in the minds of his customers.
12. To make Coca-Cola look different, Candler _____ the bottles.

B Vocabulary (new context)

Put the right word in the blanks.

themes	mass-marketing	portrayed	imitate
manufacturers	unique	promoting	modernized
logo	campaigns	advertised	image

1. The two political parties both spent millions on their political _____.

2. Egypt is _____. No other country has such a wealth of ancient monuments.
3. The _____ of that movie were that love is more powerful than money and that greed is punished.
4. Large businesses pay millions for an artist to design their _____.
5. He _____ the house by removing the old-fashioned attic and replacing it with a sun-roof.
6. Politicians spend a lot of time on platforms _____ their party ideas to the public.
7. The _____ of Chippy's Cheese also make other related products.
8. That fast-food company got ahead of their rivals with their _____ techniques. You can see them in practically every country of the world now.
9. I know they _____ their services in the Medworth newspaper because they got a lot of queries from that town.
10. He _____ himself to his employees as cold and distant, but his family said he was really warm and fun-loving.
11. This perfume has a romantic _____. It's called "Diana," and comes in a purple and gold bottle.
12. The neighbors have a parrot who can cry like a baby and meow like a cat. That bird can _____ anything.

C Vocabulary Review

Put the right word in the blanks.

receipt	puzzled	radius	proud
various	indicate	prevent	improve
traded	wherever	bills	purchases

1. One of the first exercises in math class is to learn how to measure the _____ of a circle.
2. People of _____ nationalities attended the meeting. There were Brazilians, Portuguese, some French and a few Japanese.
3. He can _____ his diet by eating more fresh vegetables and fewer fast foods.

4. The students were ———————————— when their teacher didn't arrive on time.

5. Please ——— ———————— the time of the meeting when you make the announcement.

6. Anders made several ———————————— at the supermarket before he caught the train to work.

7. "———————————— has she gone?" her friend asked, but nobody knew.

8. Can you give me the money in $10 ————————————, please?

9. She was too ———————————— to ask her family for help. She decided she'd have to get a job and finish college part time.

10. Before there was money, people ———————————— with each other.

11. That high fence is to ———————————— thieves from entering.

12. Mannfred kept the ———————————— in case he wanted to return the article later.

D Comprehension: Multiple Choice

Put a circle around the letter of the best answer.

1. Coca-Cola is sold in more than ———————————— countries around the world.
   a. 951
   b. 80
   c. 195
   d. 800

2. At first, people drank Coca-Cola as a ———————————— tonic.
   a. mass-marketed
   b. chocolate
   c. medicinal
   d. imitated

3. Coca-Cola has ———————————— of the world soft-drink market.
   a. 80%
   b. 30%
   c. 50%
   d. almost 100%

4. Candler ———————————— the original Coca-Cola bottles.
   a. modernized
   b. renewed
   c. mass marketed
   d. bought out

5. Among other places, Candler advertised his products on
   ————————————.
   a. the outside of airplanes
   b. outdoor swimming pools
   c. outdoor posters
   d. hospital walls

6. By 1902, Coca-Cola was the _____ product in the United States.
   a. cheapest
   b. best known
   c. most expensive
   d. healthiest

7. The manufacturers of Coke were the first to use _____.
   a. mass-marketing techniques
   b. soft drinks in bottles
   c. a cola-based drink
   d. themes in ads

8. Candler designed _____ logo for his product.
   a. a tongue-twisting
   b. an eye-catching
   c. a mouth-pleasing
   d. a fragile

9. Candler gave away _____ to promote Coca-Cola.
   a. the logo on the bottle
   b. time and money
   c. outdoor posters
   d. many small items

10. Coke used slogans to advertise its product. Slogans are _____.
    a. popular music
    b. catchy phrases
    c. free samples
    d. simple images

11. Candler chose _____ for his advertising campaigns.
    a. sports figures
    b. circus acrobats
    c. television comedians
    d. well known writers

12. Asa Candler bought the rights of Coca-Cola from _____.
    a. the inventor of a medicinal tonic
    b. a well known businessman
    c. a designer of logos
    d. a manufacturer

E Questions

The asterisk (*) means you have to think of the answer. You cannot find it in the text.

1. Who was the inventor of Coca-Cola?
2. In the beginning, what was it sold as?
3. Why was Pemberton willing to sell the rights of his tonic?
4. What did Candler use to make his drink popular?
*5. Can you think of products in your country that use the same technique?

6. Can you name the two changes Candler made to give his product a new look?
7. What happened when other companies tried to imitate Coca-Cola?
8. What were some of the ways that Candler advertised Coca-Cola?
9. How long has Coca-Cola been well known?
10. Who were some of the people that appeared in Coca-Cola's advertising campaigns?
11. In how many countries around the world is Coca-Cola sold?
*12. About 700,000,000 people drink a Coke every day. About how many more people would make a billion drinkers?

F Main Ideas

Which is the main idea of this chapter? Choose one.

1. Mass marketing changed Coca-Cola from a small business into a world-wide industry.
2. Coca-Cola is drunk and enjoyed in almost every country in the world.
3. Clever business deals can make an ordinary product a great one.

The Bar Code

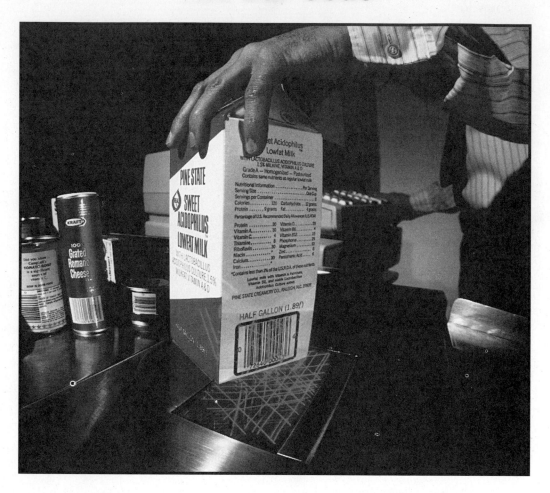

LESSON

Pre-reading Questions

1. What is this person doing with the carton of milk?

2. In what ways is your local grocery store similar to this one? In what ways is it different?

3. Can you think of any small inventions that help you in everyday life?

3

The Bar Code

What's black and white and read all over? It's smaller than a matchbox, and probably the most often seen, yet least noticed **symbol** in the United States. It helps millions of Americans
5 every day, but no one notices it. It's a few inches away from your eyes at this moment. Look at the back cover of your textbook and you'll see a **bar code.**

Bar codes are a series of black and white
10 lines of different widths. These lines **represent** the price of the product. They are "read all over" by a **scanner.** The scanner is operated by a very strong and very narrow ray of electric light called a laser beam. This beam of light
15 **translates** the black and white lines into a numbering system that the computer is able to understand. The computer **transfers** the lines into numbers, then prints the price of the product onto the screen.

20 The numbers you see at the bottom of the bar code have nothing to do with the price. They indicate which company made the product and what the item is. In supermarkets, the first six numbers say which company made the
25 product. The second six say what the product

bar code

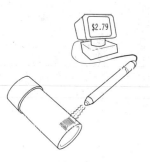

scanner

is and add a little more **information.** For example, in one supermarket, 134279 tells the computer the product is a package of cereal weighing one pound.

30 　We see **manual** scanners in small shops and bookstores or at libraries. Supermarkets have **automatic** scanners. They are underneath the glass window at the **checkout** counter. These scanners are operated by lasers

35 that look like compact discs. The disc turns around and takes in the information from the bar code in much the same way as the manual scanners do. The cashier holds the **item** over the glass window and the scanner reads all

40 the information in a few seconds. Now, shopping is a little quicker and a little easier for everyone.

　Below are some trivia points about bar codes.

45 　• Bar codes don't have to be black and white. A laser can read any color except red. (The beam of the laser is usually red in color.)

　• The bar code includes a code that alerts

50 　security if anyone tries to alter it.

　• There are some items that still don't have a bar code. No one has yet worked out a way to bar code **fragile** items like tomatoes without damaging them.

manual = by hand

automatic = by machine

checkout

A Vocabulary

Put the right word in the blanks. The sentences are from the text.

bar code	information	checkout	item
scanner	symbol	manual	automatic
represent	translates	fragile	transfers

1. The computer _____ the lines into numbers, then prints the price of the product onto the screen.
2. No one has yet worked out a way to bar code _____ items like tomatoes without damaging them.
3. The second six say what the product is and add a little more _____ .
4. Look at the back cover of your textbook and you'll see a _____ .
5. These lines _____ the price of the product.
6. This beam of light _____ the black and white lines into a numbering system that the computer is able to understand.
7. It's smaller than a matchbox, and probably the most often seen, yet least noticed _____ in the United States.
8. Supermarkets have _____ scanners.
9. They are underneath the glass window at the _____ counter.
10. They are "read all over" by a _____ .
11. The cashier holds the _____ over the glass window and the scanner reads all the information in a few seconds.
12. We see _____ scanners in small shops and bookstores or at libraries.

B Vocabulary (new context)

Put the right word in the blanks.

transfers	scanner	information	checkout
symbol	represents	translates	fragile
items	bar code	manual	automatic

1. The electric beater was broken, so we used _____ methods to mix the ingredients for the cake.

2. The wreath on the head of that statue _____ Victory.

3. Because a _____ now reads the prices and transfers them to a computer, the customers find there are fewer mistakes.

4. Reserving a seat on a plane nowadays is almost fully _____.

5. He tried to change the _____ for one on a cheaper product, but its security code alerted the store detective.

6. How many _____ of clothing did you say you're buying? You know you can only afford one.

7. There was a long line of people at the _____ waiting to pay for their supermarket purchases.

8. Jenny knew her sister would prefer the glass vase, but as it was too _____ to mail, she decided to send a book instead.

9. When you see the _____ of the knife and fork at airports, it means there is a restaurant nearby.

10. Darrel works in packing. He _____ the goods from the truck into the storehouse.

11. She's a translator. She _____ both Polish and Russian into English for international companies.

12. "I need _____ on the cacao tree," she told the librarian. "Where are the shelves with books on tropical plants?"

C Vocabulary Review

Underline the word that does not belong.

1. makers, producers, manuals, manufacturers
2. advertised, imitated, campaigned, mass marketed
3. gold, silver, metal, iron
4. various, replace, renew, modernize
5. dollars, pesos, yen, money
6. portrayed, showed, predicted, represented
7. invisible, unimportant, secondary, trivial
8. produced, traded, changed, replaced
9. manufactures, purchases, buys, shops for
10. various, precious, different, several
11. archeologists, receipts, manufacturers, experts
12. advertises, indicates, points out, shows

D Comprehension: True/False/No Information

Write T if the sentence is true. Write F if it is false. Write NI if no information is given.

1. One of the most often seen yet least noticed items in the United States is the scanner.
2. On the back cover of your textbook there is a small rectangle with a series of black and white lines.
3. There are only lines on the bar code.
4. In supermarkets, the numbers tell the computer what the price of the article is.
5. The first six numbers say what company made the product.
6. Most of the manual scanners are in supermarkets.
7. There are laser scanners that look like compact discs at the checkout counter of supermarkets.
8. The cashier passes the item underneath the counter and the scanner reads the price.
9. The laser disc takes in the information in much the same way as manual scanners do.
10. There are ten times more manual scanners than there are laser-disc scanners.
11. A laser can read most colors, but it's easier for companies to print only in black and white.
12. The bar code includes a warning that helps prevent thefts at stores and supermarkets.

E Questions

The asterisk (*) means you have to think of the answer. You cannot find it in the text.

1. What is one of the least-noticed but most often seen symbols in the United States?
2. Can you name a few places where you might find a bar code?
*3. Where is the nearest bar code to you at this moment?
4. What do bar codes consist of?
5. What does the laser beam do?
6. What are two uses for the numbers at the bottom of the bar code?

7. What do the first six numbers indicate?
8. What are the second six numbers for?
9. How many kinds of scanner are there?
10. How does the cashier operate the scanner?
11. Can bar codes be in other colors than black or white? Which color isn't any good? Why?
12. Could you place a bar code on an egg? Why? Why not?

F Main Ideas

Which is the main idea of this chapter? Choose one.

1. The bar code is a small item that makes it easier and quicker for stores to distribute goods.
2. Bar codes make goods more expensive to buy, but less easy to steal.
3. Bar codes have proved helpful in libraries as well as supermarkets.

Inflation

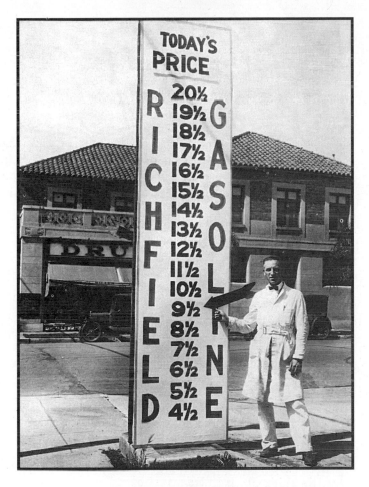

LESSON

4

Pre-reading Questions

1. Why do you think the photo was taken a long time ago?

2. What is the reason for so many different numbers?

3. What is the arrow for?

Inflation

Workers usually get paid once a week, but in Germany in the 1920s they got paid twice **daily.** Besides that, they had an extra half-hour every morning to go shopping for food. If that
5 sounds like a worker's paradise, let's see what a normal day in 1923 was really like.

     every day

At 11:30 A.M. work stopped at the factory, and Karl Hoffman lined up with the other workers. The boss gave him two huge bags. "Here's
10 your morning's **salary,**" he said. Fifty million German marks in **cash.**" Karl was in a hurry. He loaded his salary into a wheelbarrow and started to run in the **direction** of a big produce store. Inside, he joined a long line of people, all with
15 huge bags of money. "How much are the onions?" he asked the sales clerk. "Twenty-five million marks for one," she answered. Karl bought two onions and handed her the **contents** of his wheelbarrow.

     pay, wages

     what is inside

20 When Karl arrived home after the afternoon's work, his wife was cooking dinner. "I worked all morning to buy two onions," he told her. "I passed the produce store after work and goods have doubled in price. Onions now
25 cost 50 million marks each. My afternoon's salary is almost **worthless.** It will only buy one onion. I'm going to use the bills for firewood." He threw the paper money in the fire.

     without value

That incident was **typical** for millions of
30 Germans in the 1920s. People used money for
firewood. They had to work for three days to
buy a pound of butter, and twenty weeks to
buy a suit. In the chart below, you can see how
the value of the German mark dropped in just
35 nine years. In 1914, four marks equaled one
dollar. Nine years later, four trillion
(4,000,000,000,000) marks equaled one dollar.

INFLATION IN GERMANY IN THE 1920s

*The column on the right shows how many German marks were paid for one
US dollar. For example, in July 1923, one US dollar was worth 353,412
German marks.*

July 1914	4.2 marks = $1
January 1919	8.9 marks = $1
July 1919	14.0 marks = $1
January 1920	64.8 marks = $1
January 1922	191.8 marks = $1
July 1922	493.2 marks = $1
January 1923	17,972.0 marks = $1
July 1923	353,412.0 marks = $1
August 1923	4,620,455.0 marks = $1
September 1923	98,860,000.0 marks = $1
October 1923	25,260,208,000.0 marks = $1
November 1923	4,200,000,000,000.0 marks = $1

What took place during those nine years is
called runaway **inflation.** Prices rose by millions
40 of marks in a few hours. It's normal for countries
to have a little inflation, but usually it's gradual.
Prices rise by a few cents every year. For example,
in 1926 a postage stamp cost just two cents.
Today it costs over 30 cents. In **contrast** to that
45 example of normal inflation, the German
government reprinted the postage stamp again

inflation

and again. Finally, a postage stamp cost over one
million marks.

50   And what happened to Karl? He managed
to **survive.** The government changed the name
of the currency and minted new money, so
prices went down and order was **restored.**
Today the German mark is **stable,** and will   steady
probably stay that way.

A   Vocabulary

Put the right word in the blanks. The sentences are from the text.

direction	inflation	daily	worthless
typical	survive	cash	salary
stable	restored	contents	contrast

1. "Fifty million German marks in _____."
2. Karl bought two onions and handed her the _____ of
   his wheelbarrow.
3. That incident was _____ for millions of Germans in
   the 1920s.
4. Workers usually get paid once a week, but in Germany in the 1920s they
   got paid twice _____.
5. What took place during those nine years is called runaway

   _____.

6. In _____ to that example of normal inflation, the
   German government reprinted the postage stamp again and again.
7. He managed to _____.
8. Today the German mark is _____, and will probably stay
   that way.
9. The government changed the name of the currency and minted new
   money, so prices went down and order was _____.
10. He loaded his salary into a wheelbarrow and started to run in the
    _____ of a big produce store.
11. "Here's your morning's _____," he said.
12. "My afternoon's salary is almost _____."

B Vocabulary (new context)

Put the right word in the blanks.

direction	inflation	daily	worthless
typical	survive	cash	salary
stable	restored	contents	contrast

1. The Polis and their children _____ the old house and now it looks like new.
2. Tony had a serious operation; however, the doctors say he will

   _____.

3. "It was _____ of him to come to dinner with us and then not pay his share," said Magda to her friends. "He's always doing that."
4. When the price of goods rise very suddenly, it's called

   _____.

5. What _____ are you going? If you're heading toward the station, perhaps you could take me with you.
6. Lisa gets two _____ newspapers and a weekly magazine.
7. My _____ increased by 5% this year.
8. The pale grey of the walls provided an interesting _____ with the deep reds and purples of the carpet on the floor.
9. She emptied the sewing basket of its _____ and used it for shopping.
10. I'm going to the bank to get $100 in _____.
11. Most of the store goods were _____ after the flood.
12. Although their work takes them all over the place, they have a very _____ marriage.

C Vocabulary Review

Put the right word in the blanks.

manual	articles	transfers	alien
destroyed	represent	illuminated	tremendous
information	meteor	checkout	translates

1. The toy village was _____ by hundreds of tiny electric lights.
2. Bombs _____ many small villages in the last war.

3. The _____ desks at train stations will tell you what time the trains leave, but won't sell you tickets.

4. Take the groceries to the line at the _____ while I get some more fruit.

5. The railroad crossing had _____ warning systems until last year. Now they're fully automatic.

6. The ending was _____! All the cast were on stage to sing the final number.

7. The film was about a space _____ who took on human form.

8. There was a _____ shower last night. Newspapers reported there were hundreds in the sky.

9. This legal paper _____ the ownership of the car from Jim to Douglas.

10. There are two _____ written by your favorite journalist in this magazine.

11. Pilar works for a company in the Philippines. She _____ business contracts into Japanese.

12. I don't know who will _____ him in court. All I know is that he needs someone to defend him.

D Comprehension: Sequence

Number these sentences in the right order. The first is done for you.

_____ He stopped when he got to the produce store.

_____ The boss gave Karl two huge bags and told him they were his salary.

_____ He told his wife that prices had doubled since the morning.

_____ There was a long line of people waiting inside the produce store.

_____ He bought two onions.

_____ Karl Hoffman lined up with the other workers.

_____ He threw his morning's salary into the fire.

_____ He went back to work and left at the usual time.

___1___ Work stopped at the factory at 11:30 A.M.

_____ His wife was cooking dinner when he got home.

_____ Karl asked how much the onions were and learned that they cost twenty-five million German marks each.

_____ Karl loaded his salary onto a wheelbarrow and started running.

E Questions

The asterisk (*) means you have to think of the answer. You cannot find it in the text.

1. What was unusual about how workers were paid in Germany in the 1920s?
2. How much time did a worker have for shopping in 1923?
*3. Can you name some types of workers who might get time off for shopping in your country today?
4. In 1923, what would fifty million German marks buy in the morning?
5. What would it buy in the afternoon?
6. What did Karl Hoffman do with his morning's salary?
7. What did he do with his salary in the afternoon?
8. Look at the chart. How much was a German mark worth against the American dollar in July 1914? How much was a German mark worth in November 1923?
9. How much did a postage stamp cost in the United States in 1926? How much does it cost today?
*10. Do you know any countries that have inflation?

F Main Ideas

Which is the main idea of this chapter? Choose one.

1. In November, 1923, an American dollar was worth over a trillion German marks.
2. Inflation was so bad in Germany in the 1920s that workers got paid twice a day.
3. Inflation can cause a country's economy to collapse.

Doing Business Around the World

LESSON

Pre-reading Questions

1. Where do you think the man in photo A is going?

2. What are the men doing in photo B? In what other ways do people greet each other?

3. What are the people eating with in photo C? Would it be hard or easy for you to eat like this? Why?

Doing Business Around the World

There are different **customs** in different parts of the world. For example, how would you say the date 2-1-1999? Many South Americans give the answer as the second of January, 1999.
5 They put the day before the month. But North Americans give the answer as February the first. They put the month before the day. When they're in another country, business people sometimes miss meetings because they **confuse**
10 the various ways of writing dates.

If someone nods their head up and down, what does it mean to you? "No" or "yes"? Nodding the head up and down means "yes" in Europe and the United States, but "no" in
15 Greece and Turkey. The difference only confuses the tourist, but to business people it sometimes means losing a **contract.** To prevent misunderstandings, some business people attend classes or read books to learn about the
20 different manners and customs of other countries. They don't want to lose a contract by offending their **clients.**

Both classes and books show that what are good manners in one country are sometimes bad
25 manners in another. Even simple **gestures** can have different meanings. The "thumbs-up" sign means "excellent" in the United States, but it's an

ways of behaving

an agreement, usually signed by the people making it.

gestures

insult in parts of Africa. Tapping the head with the forefinger in parts of South America means "I'm thinking hard," but in Holland it means "that's crazy." To point a finger at someone is okay in Canada, but it's rude in Japan.

Greeting clients correctly makes a good first **impression.** European men and women generally shake hands when meeting for the first time, but in Arab countries men never shake hands with women they're not related to. In Japan, people bow to each other. People from India place their hands together as if praying, then bow the head.

In business, **entertaining** is important. It's a good idea to invite a client out to eat. However, unless the host is careful, dining out can be a problem. There are many food **taboos.** Some people are vegetarian; others don't drink alcohol. In the West, people eat with knives and forks; in the East, they eat with chopsticks.

things that are forbidden

Sometimes business **executives** are invited into the homes of their clients. It's the custom in most countries for the guest to take a small gift to the host. Even here there are rules. In England giving a knife is bad luck. The Chinese refuse a gift three times before accepting it, because they do not want to appear greedy. Some people in southeast Asia don't give handkerchiefs because it makes them think of crying at funerals. One of the biggest difficulties is how much to spend. If the guest spends only a little, the host might think the gift is stingy. If the guest spends too much, the host might think the gift is a **bribe.** In Malaysia and many other countries, there are strict rules against bribery.

a business manager with extra powers

If you ever see a worried-looking **foreigner** in a gift shop, he or she is probably a business executive wondering what to buy.

A Vocabulary

Put the right word in the blanks. The sentences are from the text.

contract	insult	taboos	entertaining
executives	impression	confuse	clients
customs	gestures	bribe	foreigner

1. The difference only confuses the tourist, but to business people it sometimes means losing a _____.
2. The "thumbs-up" sign means "excellent" in the United States, but it's an _____ in parts of Africa.
3. Greeting clients correctly makes a good first _____.
4. Even simple _____ can have different meanings.
5. If you ever see a worried looking _____ in a gift shop, it's probably a business executive wondering what to buy.
6. There are different _____ in different parts of the world.
7. There are many food _____.
8. They don't want to lose a contract by offending their _____.
9. If the guest spends too much, the host might think the gift is a _____.
10. When they're in another country, business people sometimes miss meetings because they _____ the various ways of writing dates.
11. Sometimes business _____ are invited into the homes of their clients.
12. In business, _____ is important.

B Vocabulary (new context)

Put the right word in the blanks.

executives	impression	confuse	customs
gestures	bribe	foreigner	insult
clients	entertaining	contract	taboos

1. In some parts of the world, there are very strict _____ about men and women bathing together. Women must bathe in a separate pool.
2. The singers are _____ the audience with some folk songs.

3. Tourists often _____ the coins of the country they're traveling in.

4. The lawyer was very hard working and soon had many new

_____ .

5. The business _____ of the chemical company attended a meeting last July.

6. He gave the _____ he had lots of money but both Julia and Margarita thought he was actually very poor.

7. Those _____ the customs' officer is making means that we're to open our suitcases.

8. Before the client signed the _____ his lawyers looked it over very carefully.

9. It's better not to accept that expensive gift. I think it's a

_____ .

10. You could tell he was a _____ . He had to ask for help in buying a train ticket.

11. No, don't wave like that! In this country holding five fingers in the air is an _____ .

12. Iran has some very interesting _____ . On the last day of their New Year the men jump over a fire.

C Vocabulary Review

Match the words with the word or phrase that means the same. One is done for you.

Column A

1. inflation _____o_____
2. daily _____
3. worthless _____
4. solemn _____
5. stable _____
6. contrast _____
7. fragile _____
8. cash _____
9. survive _____
10. uncommon _____
11. illuminated _____
12. alien _____

Column B

a. serious
b. steady
c. paper money and coins
d. entertaining
e. rare
f. lit
g. difference
h. foreign
i. every day
j. easily broken
k. ruined
l. slowly

13. destroyed   _____   m. continue to live
14. gradually   _____   n   valueless
                                  o. price increase

D Comprehension: Multiple Choice

Put a circle around the letter of the best answer.

1. A very expensive gift might be taken for a _____.
    a. business deal   c. bribe
    b. funeral   d. taboo

2. The Chinese refuse a gift before they finally accept it, because they do not want to appear _____.
    a. solemn   c. stingy
    b. greedy   d. too happy

3. Business people learn about the customs of the country they're going to visit, because they don't want to _____ their clients.
    a. offend   c. please
    b. bribe   d. do business with

4. _____ can have different meanings in different countries.
    a. business   c. clients
    b. gestures   d. purchases

5. Tapping the head with the forefinger means "_____" in Holland.
    a. that's clever   c. that's crazy
    b. that's a bribe   d. I'm thinking hard

6. If you greet people politely, it makes a good first _____.
    a. bribe   c. difficulty
    b. entertainment   d. impression

7. In England, some people say that giving a knife is _____.
    a. bad luck   c. good luck
    b. a bribe   d. a contract

8. _____ make people think of funerals in some parts of southeast Asia.
    a. knives   c. bribes
    b. eating with chopsticks d. handkerchiefs

9. When business executives travel to foreign countries, they are sometimes invited into the homes of their _____.
   a. guests
   b. clients
   c. business people
   d. tourist agents

10. Many people are _____. They don't eat meat.
    a. business people
    b. guests
    c. hosts
    d. vegetarians

E Questions

The asterisk (*) means you have to think of the answer. You cannot find it in the text.

1. How do you write the thirteenth of July, 1948, in figures in South America?
2. How do you write the twentieth of December, 1948, in figures in the United States?
*3. How do you usually write the thirtieth of April, 1948, in figures in your country?
4. How do people indicate "yes" in the United States? How do people indicate "no" in Turkey?
*5. How do you indicate "yes" in your country?
6. What do people in Europe usually do when meeting for the first time?
7. Do people in Arab countries shake hands with women they've never met? *Why do you think this is?
8. What do people in Japan do when meeting for the first time?
9. Name a food taboo.
10. What do people eat with in China?
11. What would you not take as a gift when invited out in England? *Why do you think this is?
12. What do the Chinese do before accepting a gift? Why?

F Main Ideas

Which is the main idea of this chapter? Choose one.

1. It can be difficult to do business in foreign countries.
2. It's a good idea to learn the customs of a place before doing business there.
3. There are many strange and interesting customs in the countries of the world.

Word Study

A Gerunds

A gerund is the *-ing* form of a verb. The **boldfaced** words in the examples below are gerunds.

> *Example:* Michy spends a lot of time **sleeping**.
> When she is not asleep, she enjoys **looking** out the window and **catching** mice.

We often use a gerund after these verbs and expressions:

enjoy	remember	spend time
don't mind	finish	spend money
dislike	stop	start

Write the gerund form of these verbs.

Verb	Gerund	Verb	Gerund
promote	_____	sell	_____
imitate	_____	shop	_____
read	_____	use	_____
watch	_____	talk	_____
insult	_____	spend	_____

Choose a gerund from the list above to complete each sentence.

1. Pemberton didn't mind _____ Coca-Cola because it wasn't selling very well.
2. Candler spent a lot of time _____ Coca-Cola.
3. A lot of people enjoy _____ in big stores.
4. I don't mind _____ money on something well made.
5. Do you remember _____ that book about inflation?
6. A lot of people, myself included, dislike _____ ads on TV.
7. Do you know when people started _____ coins for money?
8. Soft drink companies stopped _____ Coca-Cola when Candler took them to court.

9. That shopkeeper enjoys _____ his customers. Soon he won't have any left.

10. I don't remember _____ to him on the telephone.

B Adjectives with *-ive*

Add the suffix *-ive* to these verbs to form adjectives. Write the adjectives in the blanks.

Verb	Adjective
object	_____
invent	_____
express	_____
support	_____

Drop the final *-e* on these verbs and than add the suffix *-ive*. Write the adjectives in the blanks.

Verb	Adjective
alternate	_____
indicate	_____
negate	_____

Drop the final *-e* on these verbs and than add *-ative*. Write the adjectives in the blanks.

Verb	Adjective
represent	_____
inform	_____
imagine	_____
compare	_____

C Word Forms

	Verb	Noun	Adjective
1.	symbolize	symbol	symbolic
2.	imitate	imitation	
3.	promote	promotion	
4.	advertise	advertisement	
5.	translate	translation	

	Verb	**Noun**	**Adjective**
6.	inform	information	informative
7.	direct	direction	
8.	entertain	entertainment	entertaining
9.	confuse	confusion	confusing
10.	survive	survival	surviving

Put the correct word form in the blanks. Use a word from Line 1 in Sentence 1, and so on. Use the right verb forms and singular and plural nouns.

1. The _____ of peace is a dove. The unicorn
   _____ purity. The dove and the unicorn
   are _____ animals.
2. Her _____ of Shirley is very good. I wish I was
   able to _____ people like she does.
3. Damion's company _____ him to president. He
   talked about his _____ for weeks on end.
4. The Coca-Cola company _____ its product on
   posters, walls and barns. These _____ attracted a lot
   of attention.
5. Juanita _____ the story from French to Spanish.
   Unfortunately, her _____ wasn't very good and no
   one was able to understand it.
6. The professor left some _____ out. He wasn't able to
   _____ us about the latest events because he left
   China three years ago.
7. I gave _____ to their house but Katie lost them.
   Luckily, a policeman was able to _____ her there.
8. They _____ us with some pieces from a well-known
   musical comedy. I love that form of _____.
9. A lot of people _____ me and my brother. This
   _____ doesn't surprise me, because we look alike.
10. Their _____ depended on collecting enough food for
    winter. Otherwise they wouldn't _____.

D Past Tense Review

Write the past tense of these verbs.

1. promote	5. produce	9. play
2. sell	6. predict	10. pay
3. spend	7. confuse	11. send
4. vary	8. write	12. hear

E Writing

Choose one or more of the topics and write answers.

1. In your opinion, was Asa Candler a good businessman? Why or why not?
2. Tell about an imaginary shopping experience in the year 2025. Describe the shops, the goods, and how you will pay for them.
3. Imagine that the experts are predicting runaway inflation for the near future. What are you going to do to prepare for it? Describe your actions.

Video Highlights

A Before You Watch

1. Look at the photo to the right and discuss these questions.

   a. Do you know the product advertised in the picture? How?
   b. Is there another similar product that can compete with it?

2. These words will help you understand the video. Read the words and their definitions.

©CNN

   a. estimate: to make a judgment about something, to guess
   b. international: of or about two or more nations
   c. script: writing
   d. double digits: anything from 10 to 99
   e. sponsor: a group or business that helps pay for something

Now choose one of the key words above for each of these sentences. Some words may be used twice. You will hear similar sentences in the video.

   a. The familiar red-and-white _____ can be seen in subway stations and street corners all over the world.
   b. It's an _____ company and an _____ drink.
   c. Sales will jump by _____ in Europe.
   d. Coca-Cola was a _____ for the Olympic Games in Atlanta.
   e. Coke _____ that people drink 38 million gallons worldwide each day.

B As You Watch

1. You will hear some place names in the video. Put a check next to the ones you hear.

_____ a. Cairo (Egypt)   _____ f. Central America
_____ b. Eastern Europe   _____ g. Atlanta (United States)
_____ c. South America   _____ h. China
_____ d. Russia   _____ i. Australia
_____ e. Middle East   _____ j. Africa

2. Some of the scenes below are in the video. Check the ones you see.

		No	Yes
a.	crates of Coca-Cola with the logo	_____	_____
b.	young people drinking Coke	_____	_____
c.	a couple fighting over who gets the last Coke	_____	_____
d.	the Coca-Cola script	_____	_____
e.	a man walking a dog with the Coke logo behind him	_____	_____
f.	an ice-skater spinning on a can of Coke	_____	_____
g.	the Coke logo on the cover of a magazine	_____	_____
h.	a dog running away with a baby's can of Coke	_____	_____

C After You Watch

1. Part of the video was about the choice of the city for the 1996 Olympic Games. Athens, Greece, the home of the first Olympic Games, and Atlanta, U.S., the home of Coca-Cola, were the two main opponents. Below, two officials argue about their cities. One is from Athens and one from Atlanta. Decide which official is speaking, then write the name of the city in the space provided. They are not taking turns to speak.

_____ official: My city is the home of the Olympics. We played in the first Olympic Games thousands of years ago.

_____ official: My city is the home of Coca-Cola. It has offered millions of dollars if we get the games.

_____ official: My city has lots of money.

_____ official: My city has lots of history.

_____ official: We have stadiums which are thousands of years old.

_____ official: We can build stadiums which cost millions of dollars.

Many other countries were not happy when Atlanta won. They felt that Coca-Cola had bought the Olympic Games to advertise its product. Which side are you on? Do you think sponsors are a good idea? Add two more reasons under the side you choose.

For Sponsors: *I think it's great to have sponsors for the Olympic Games. They can help poor athletes buy equipment.*

Against Sponsors: *I think sponsors for the Olympic Games are a bad idea. The athletes they help have to advertise the company products.*

_____   _____
_____   _____
_____   _____
_____   _____

_____   _____
_____   _____
_____   _____

Activity Page

Business Crossword

Across

1. You have to _____ questions to get answers.
4. Where you pay for goods in a supermarket.
6. Everybody recognizes the Coca-Cola _____.
7. Texas is the largest in the mainland U.S.
9. Signed agreements.
12. Payment for work.
14. Short for Chief Executive Officer.
15. Wise people do it with answer to 12 across.

Down

2. Another name for a shop.
3. Business people study them before they visit a foreign country.
4. Short for Cash On Delivery.
5. What you need when you pay for something.
8. How often do people pay income tax? (two words: 5, 4)
9. Customer.
10. Employers set them and employees obey them.
11. Business people often _____ to foreign countries.
13. Short for As Soon As Possible.

Dictionary Page

Capitalization and Abbreviation

Both capitalization and abbreviations are often used in business. Most trademarks (Coca-Cola, Toyota, Kodak, etc.) are capitalized, and many are abbreviated (IBM, BP, Aramco).

1. **Capitalization** Your dictionary shows when a word needs capital letters. Look at the entries below. Circle the entry that is capitalized. In the middle entry, count the number of capital letters that come after **USAGE NOTE.** Put the number in the circle.

afraid /əˈfreɪd/ *adjective*
fearful: *The child is afraid of dogs and cries everytime one comes close by.*

African-American /ˈæfrɪkən/ *noun*
an American whose ancestors were African: *He is an African-American.* *—adjective* **African-American.** *See:* black.

USAGE NOTE: Compare *African-American* and *black.* In the USA, the terms *African-American* and *black* are both used to talk about Americans of African descent. Some people use the term *African-American*, other prefer the term *black.* Both are acceptable. ◯

---

after /ˈæftər/ *preposition*
1 in back of, behind: *I told my dog to stay home, but he came after me.*
2 later in time: *We had dinner after the movie.*
after *conjunction*
later than: *She came to the party after I did. (antonym)* before.

2. **Abbreviation** This is a short or abbreviated form of a word or words. Abbreviations do not have to be capitalized. Underline the abbreviations in the dictionary entries below. Which of the underlined entries do you think are the most useful to business people? Circle five or six.

ATM
abbreviation of automated teller machine

ID or ID card /ˈaɪˈdiː/ *noun*
abbreviation of identity card.

C.O.D. or COD /ˌsioʊˈdi/ *noun*
abbreviation of cash on delivery, meaning that one pays the person who delivers the goods for the goods, and for the cost of sending them: *I paid for the shoes C.O.D.*

ASAP or asap
abbreviation of as soon as possible: *Call me ASAP.*

GNP /ˌdʒiɛnˈpi/ *noun*
abbreviation of gross national product.

elsewhere /ˈɛlsˌwɛr/ *adverb*
in some other place: *She doesn't live here; she must live elsewhere.*

ELT /ˌiˌɛlˈti/
abbreviation of English Language Teaching

E-mail or e-mail /ˈiˌmeɪl/ *noun*
short for electronic mail

nearby *adverb*
close: *Is there a post office nearby?*

ad /æd/ *noun informal*
short for advertisement

afford /əˈfɔrd/ *verb*
to be able to do or pay for something: *We can't afford to buy that expensive car; we don't have enough money.*

CD /ˌsiˈdi/ *noun*
abbreviation of compact disc: *I bought two new CDs today.*

IOU /ˈaɪoʊˈyu/
abbreviation of I owe you: a written promise to pay back money

IPA /ˈaɪpiˈei/
abbreviation of International Phonetic Alphabet

U.N. /ˌyuˈɛn/ *noun*
abbreviation of the United Nations

In the space provided, write in the missing abbreviation.

1. He quickly wrote out an ————————— for the missing money. (IOU, ASAP, ID)
2. Please give me an answer —————————. (GNP, IPA, ASAP)
3. Jenny put an ————————— in the newspapers for her secondhand bicycle. (ad, COD, ID)
4. The ————————— of that country rose by 10% in two years. (ATM, U.N., GNP)
5. I have no cash. I'll have to go to the ————————— after work. (A.M., ATM, ID)

Vocabulary

row 5
royalty 21
rushes 56

S
sacred 85
salary 192
scanner 185
scarce 98
seems 21
seldom 97
series 56
settled 136
shatters 130
sidewalk 46
similar 61
slide fastener 5
smoothes 46
snack 91
solemn 143
solid 92
solve 124
source 103
species 79
stable 194
statues 143
steps aside 56
straight 46

strips 5
substitute 104
sumo wrestling 56
supernatural 131
supports 103
survive 194
swings 46
symbol 185

T
taboos 200
term 85
themes 178
theory 144
touches 56
tournaments 56
traded 170
train 51
transfers 185
translates 185
tremendous 149
tribes 21
trivia 171
typical 193

U
unfortunately 136
unique 177

untrue 97
unusual 131

V
valleys 61
valued 91
vanished 136
various 171
vegetarian 104

W
weapons 41
whatever 16
wherever 61
worthless 192
wouldn't 21

Y
yells 46

Z
zipper 5

Skills Index

Irregular Verbs

Simple	Past	Simple	Past
be	was, were	hear	heard
become	became	hit	hit
begin	began	hurt	hurt
blow	blew	keep	kept
bring	brought	know	knew
build	built	lead	led
buy	bought	leave	left
catch	caught	lose	lost
choose	chose	make	made
come	came	meet	met
cut	cut	pay	paid
do (does)	did	put	put
drink	drank	ring	rang
drive	drove	run	ran
eat	ate	see	saw
fall	fell	sell	sold
feel	felt	send	sent
fight	fought	sleep	slept
find	found	slide	slid
fly	flew	speak	spoke
forget	forgot	spend	spent
freeze	froze	sweep	swept
get	got	take	took
give	gave	teach	taught
go (goes)	went	tell	told
grow	grew	think	thought
have (has)	had	understand	understood
		wear	wore
		win	won
		write	wrote

ARCTIC
OCEAN

GREENLAND

Alaska (U.S.)

Baffin
Bay

Yukon
Territory

Northwest Territories

British
Columbia

Alberta

CANADA

Manitoba

Hudson
Bay

Saskatchewan

Newfoundland

Ontario

Quebec

Washington

Prince
Edward
Island

Oregon

Montana

North Dakota

Minnesota

New Hampshire
Vermont

New
Brunswick

Idaho

Maine

Nova
Scotia

Wyoming

South Dakota

Nevada

Wisconsin

Massachusetts

Utah

Nebraska

Iowa

Michigan

New York

Rhode Island
Connecticut

UNITED   STATES

Illinois

Indiana

Ohio

Pennsylvania

New Jersey
Maryland

California

Colorado

Kansas

West
Virginia

Virginia

Delaware
Washington D.C.

Arizona

Missouri

Kentucky

North Carolina

New Mexico

Oklahoma

Arkansas

Tennessee

South Carolina

ATLANTIC
OCEAN

Texas

Mississippi

Alabama

Georgia

Louisiana

PACIFIC
OCEAN

Florida

MEXICO

Gulf of Mexico

Hawaii

PUERTO
RICO

NORTH

WEST   EAST

SOUTH

222

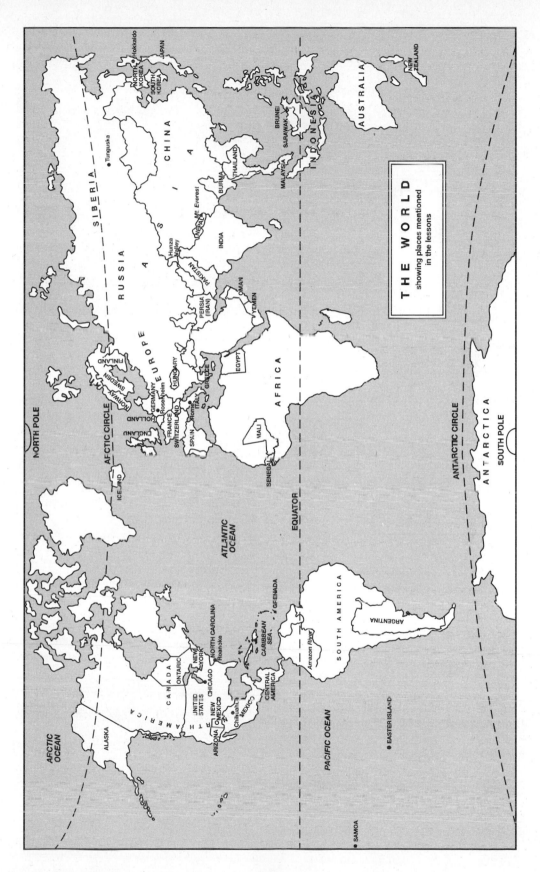

THE WORLD
showing places mentioned
in the lessons

NORTH POLE

ARCTIC OCEAN

ALASKA

ARCTIC CIRCLE

CANADA

AMERICA

ONTARIO

NEW YORK

UNITED STATES

CHICAGO

ARIZONA

NEW MEXICO

MEXICO

Chihuahua

NORTH CAROLINA

Roanoke

CENTRAL AMERICA

CARIBBEAN SEA

GRENADA

ICELAND

ATLANTIC OCEAN

EQUATOR

SOUTH AMERICA

Amazon River

ARGENTINA

PACIFIC OCEAN

EASTER ISLAND

SAMOA

ANTARCTIC CIRCLE

ANTARCTICA

SOUTH POLE

NORWAY

SWEDEN

FINLAND

EUROPE

HOLLAND

ENGLAND

GERMANY

Rosenheim

FRANCE

SWITZERLAND

HUNGARY

ITALY

Rome

GREECE

SPAIN

MALI

SENEGAL

EGYPT

AFRICA

YEMEN

OMAN

PERSIA (IRAN)

PAKISTAN

Hunza Valley

NEPAL

Mt. Everest

INDIA

RUSSIA

SIBERIA

Tunguska

ASIA

CHINA

NORTH KOREA

SOUTH KOREA

JAPAN

Hokkaido

BURMA

THAILAND

MALAYSIA

BRUNEI

SARAWAK

INDONESIA

AUSTRALIA

NEW ZEALAND

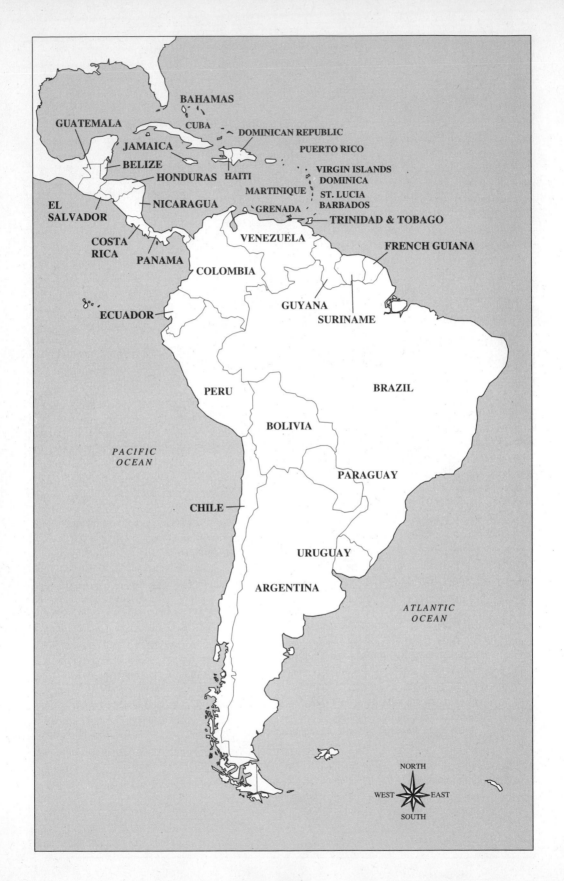

BAHAMAS

GUATEMALA

CUBA

DOMINICAN REPUBLIC

JAMAICA

PUERTO RICO

BELIZE

VIRGIN ISLANDS

HONDURAS

HAITI

DOMINICA

MARTINIQUE

ST. LUCIA

EL
SALVADOR

NICARAGUA

GRENADA

BARBADOS

TRINIDAD & TOBAGO

VENEZUELA

FRENCH GUIANA

COSTA
RICA

PANAMA

COLOMBIA

ECUADOR

GUYANA

SURINAME

PACIFIC
OCEAN

PERU

BRAZIL

BOLIVIA

PARAGUAY

CHILE

URUGUAY

ARGENTINA

ATLANTIC
OCEAN

NORTH

WEST   EAST

SOUTH

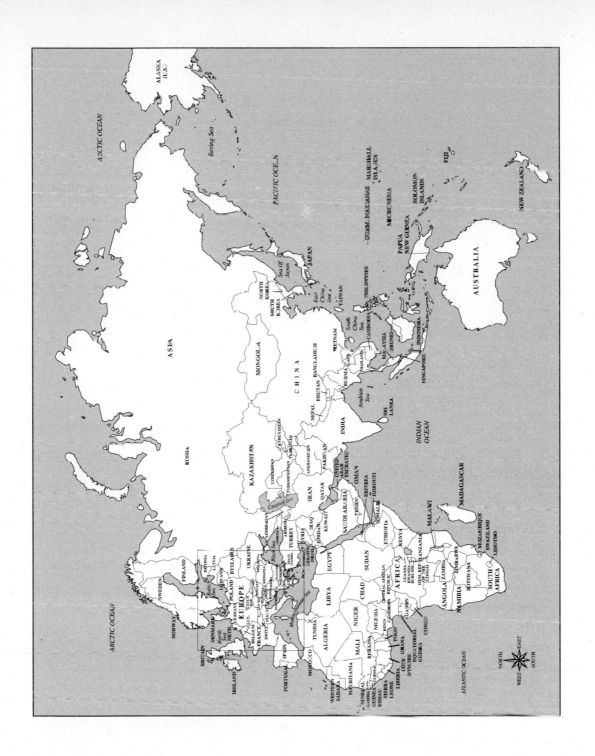